DANIEL RUCZKO

CHRISTMAS NIGHTMARE

A collection of Christmas-themed horror images inspired by the look of comic books from the 80s.

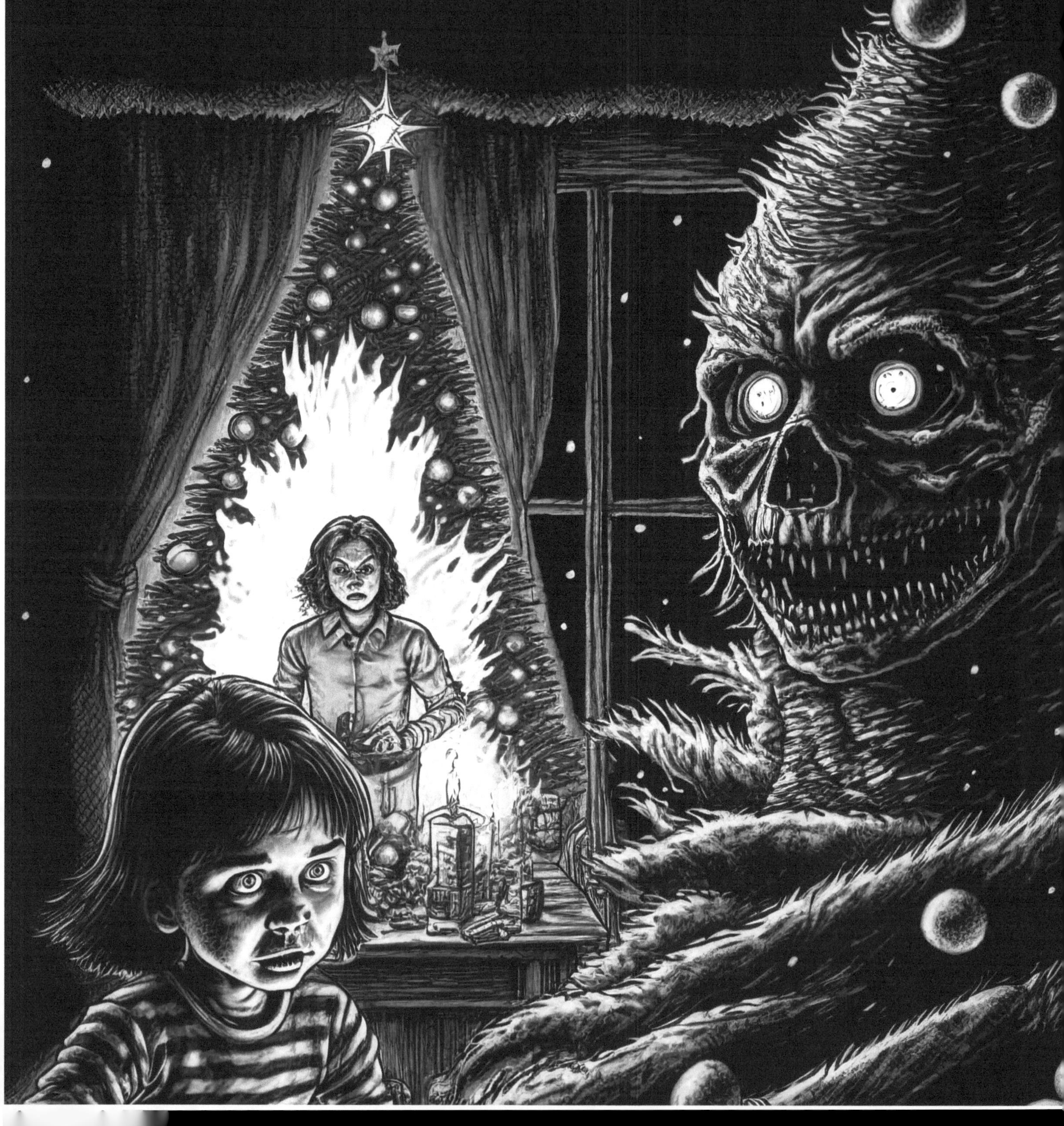

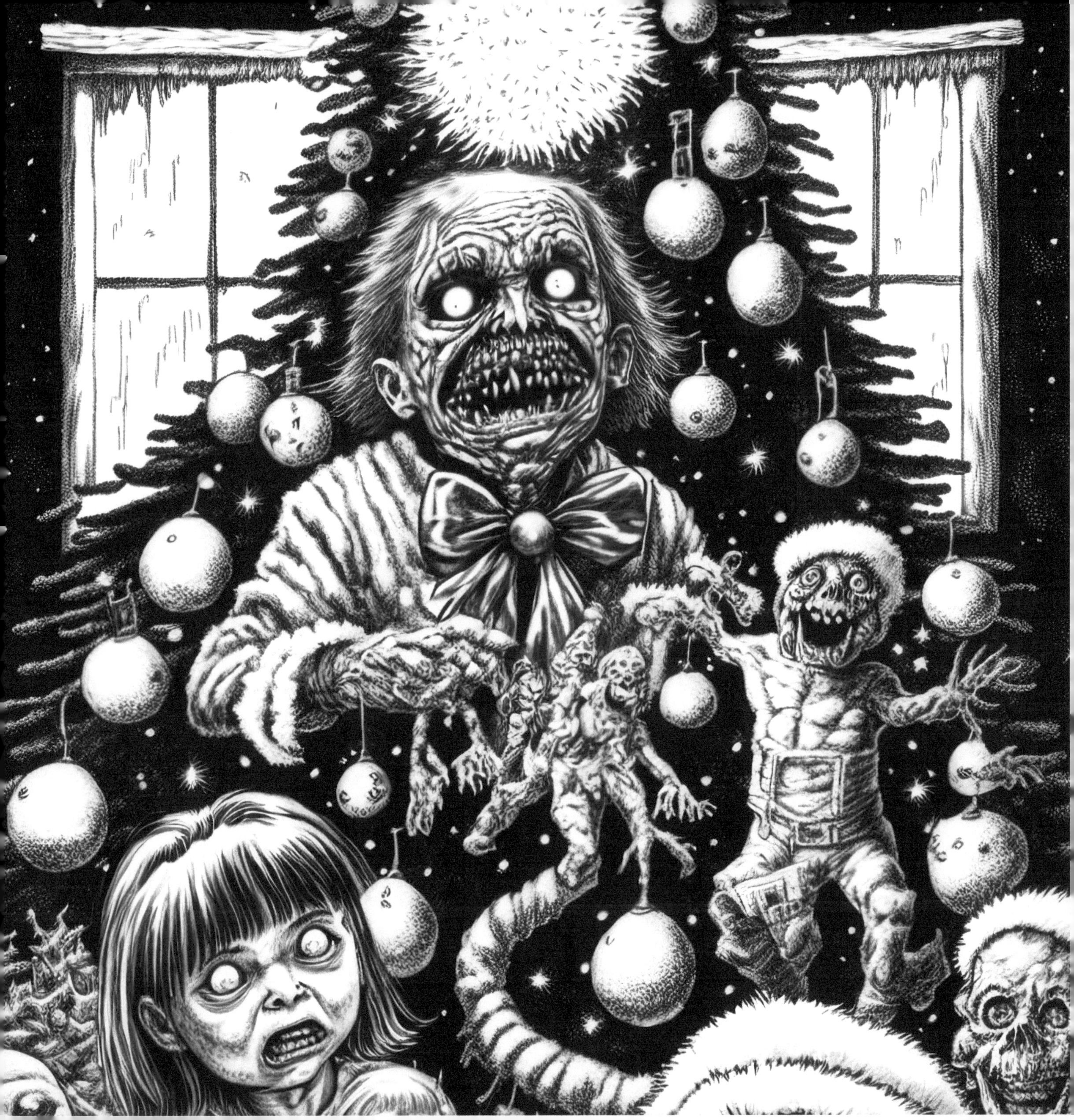

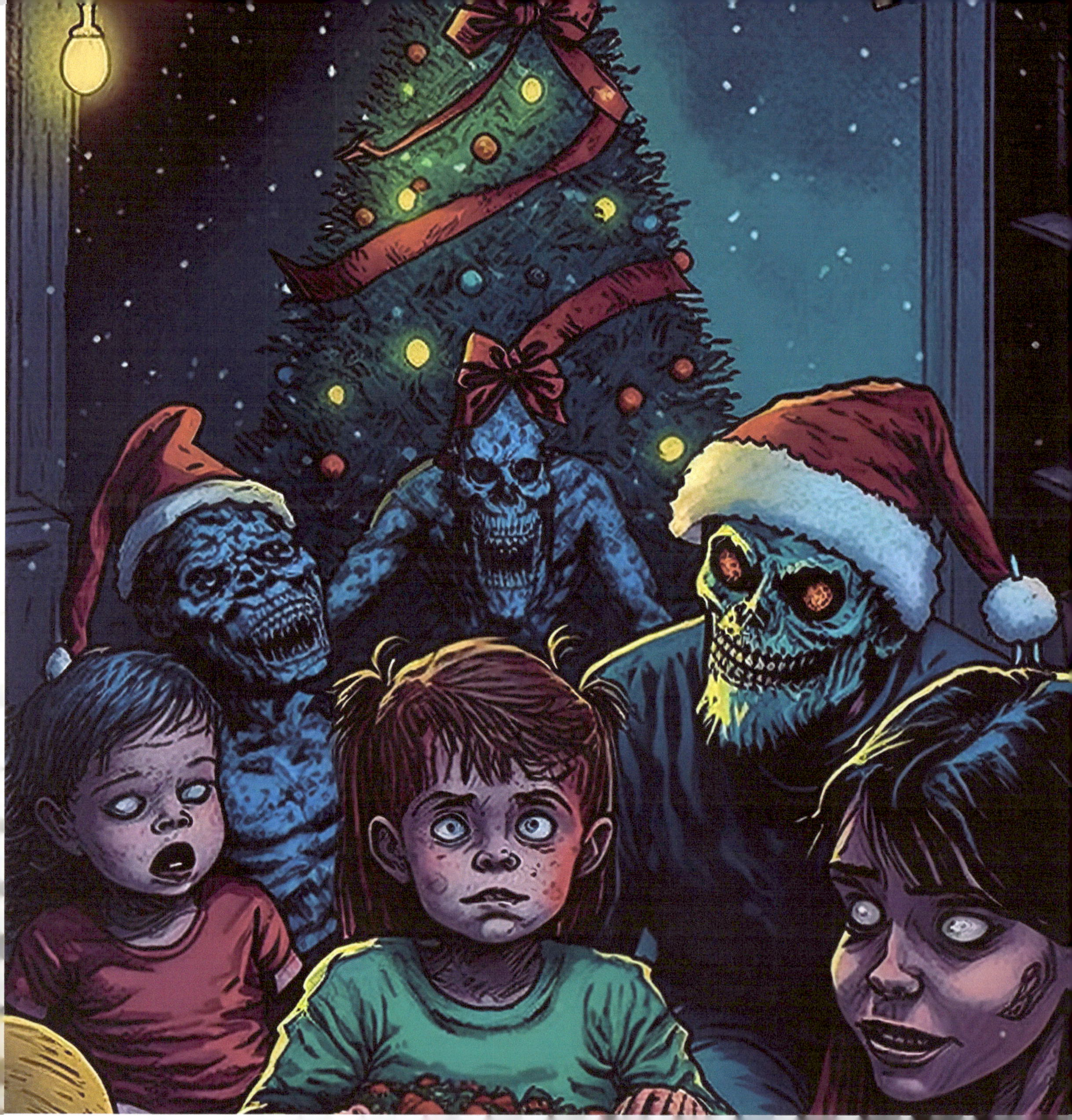

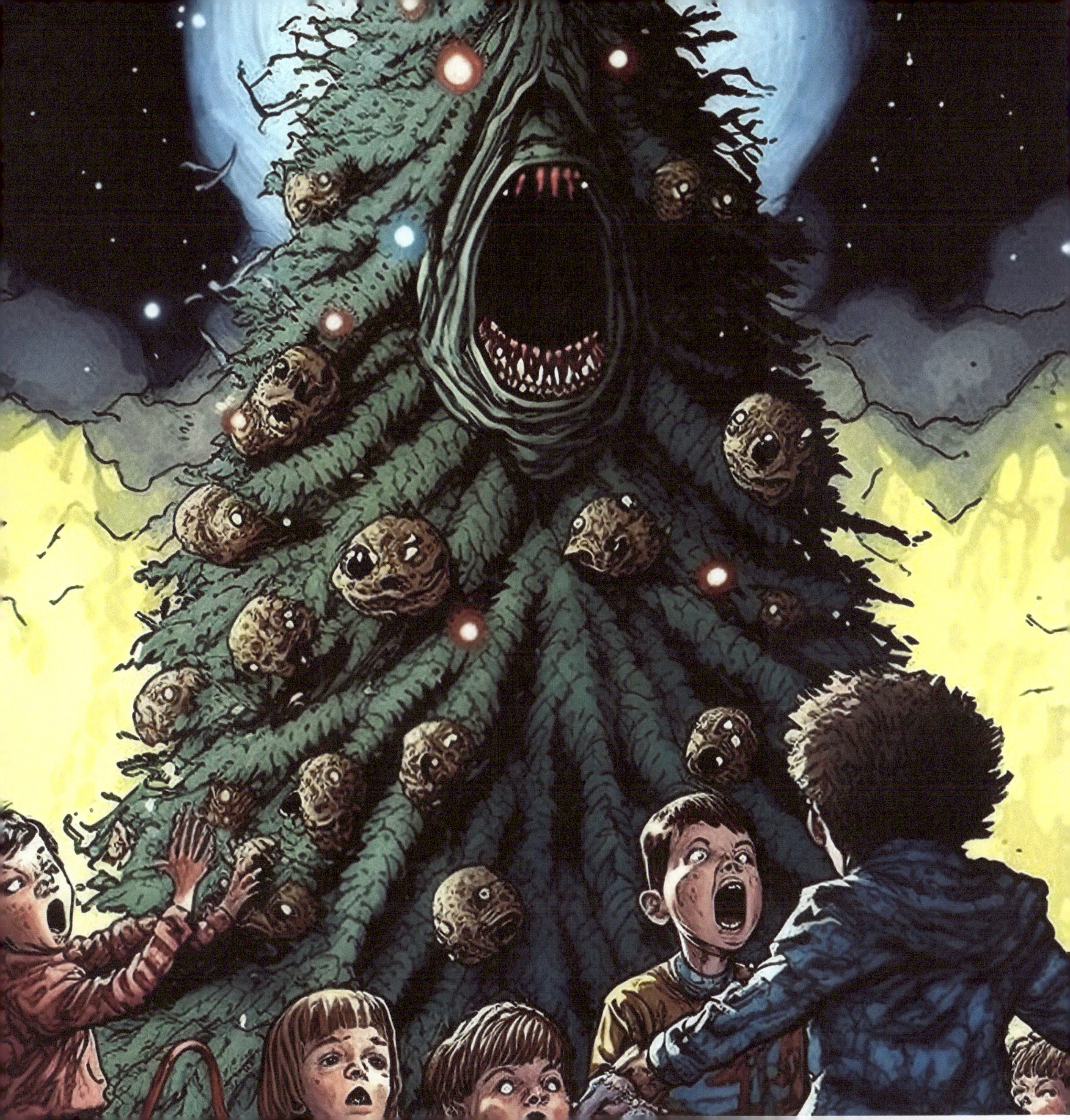

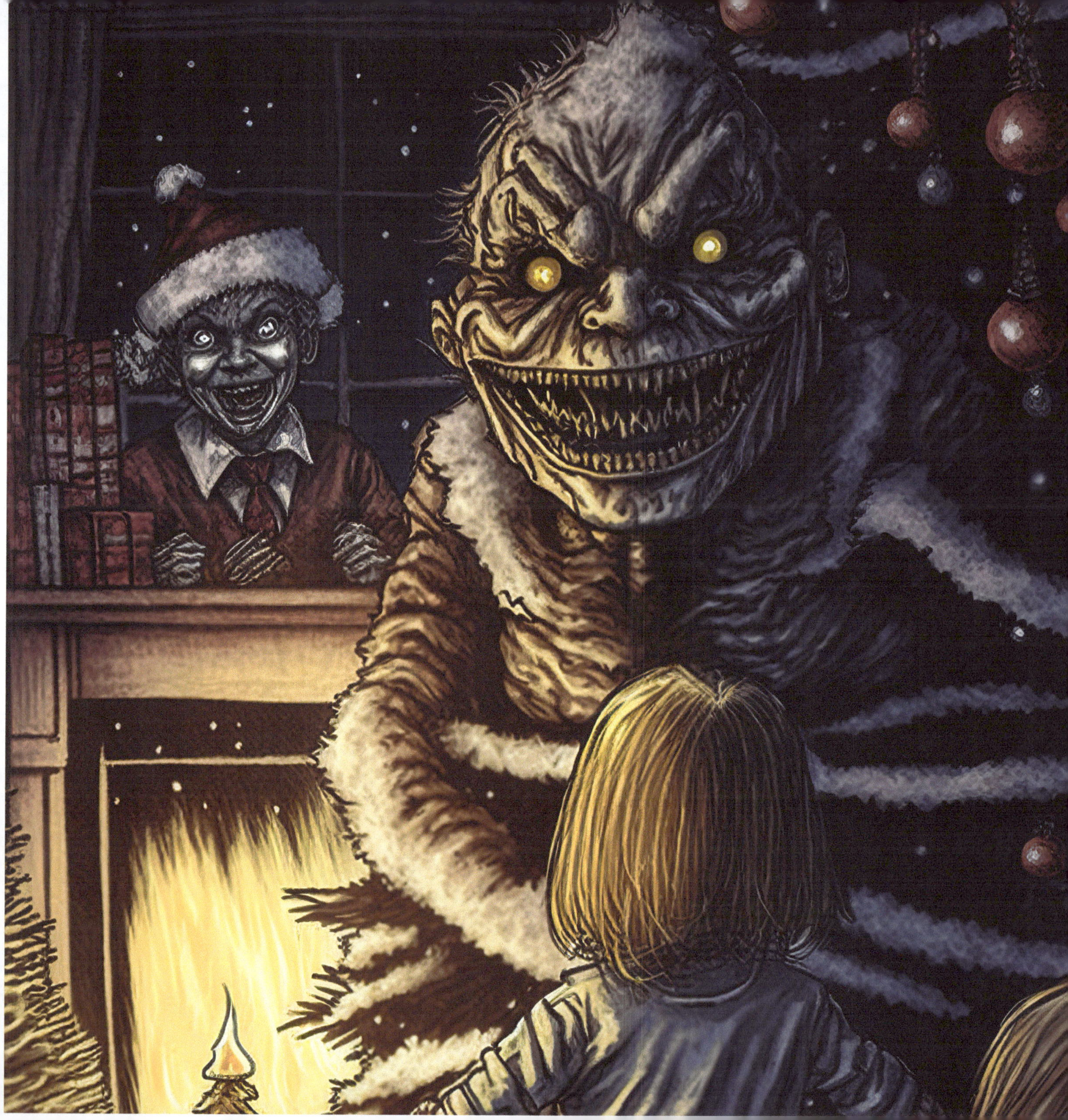

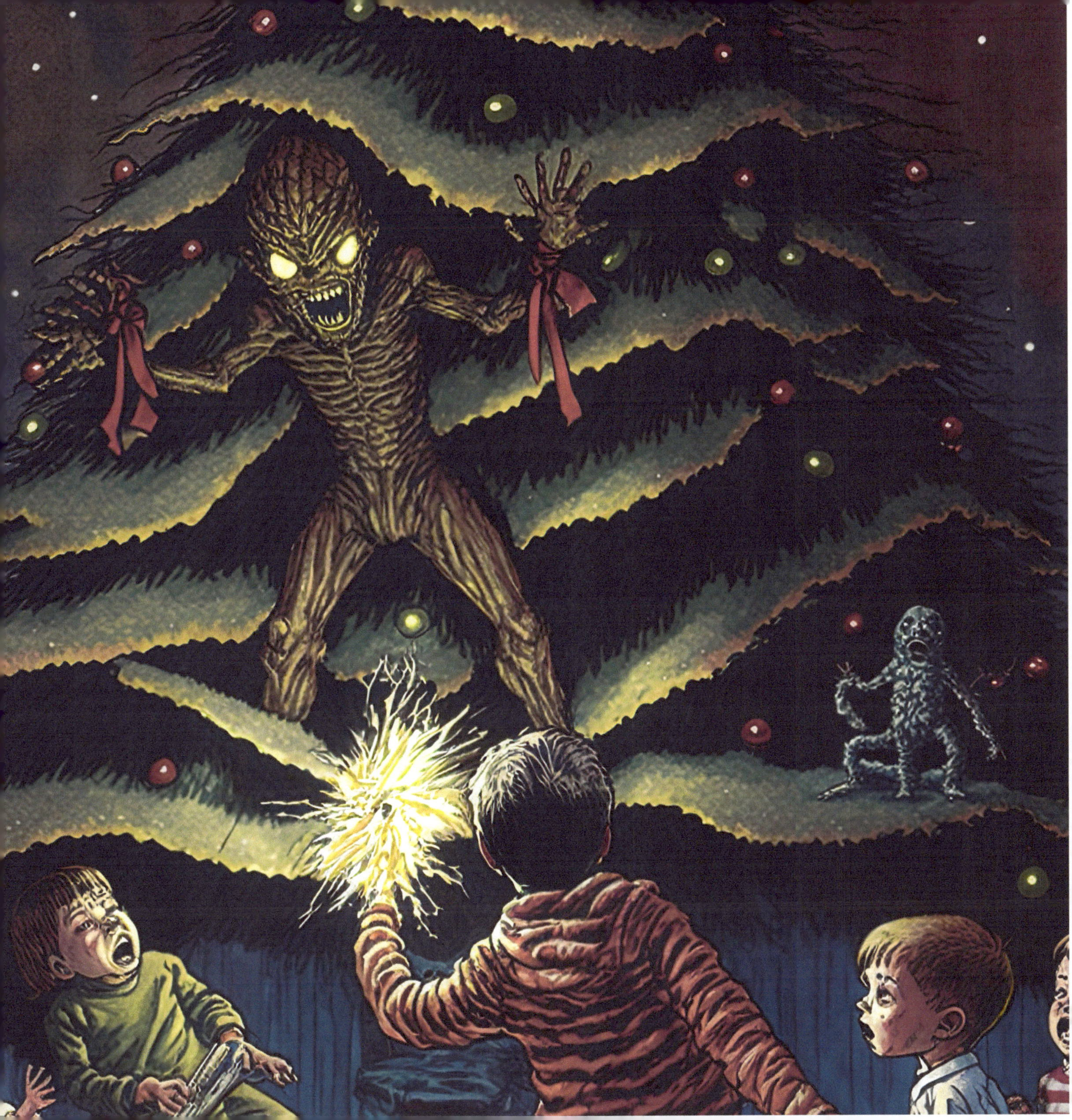

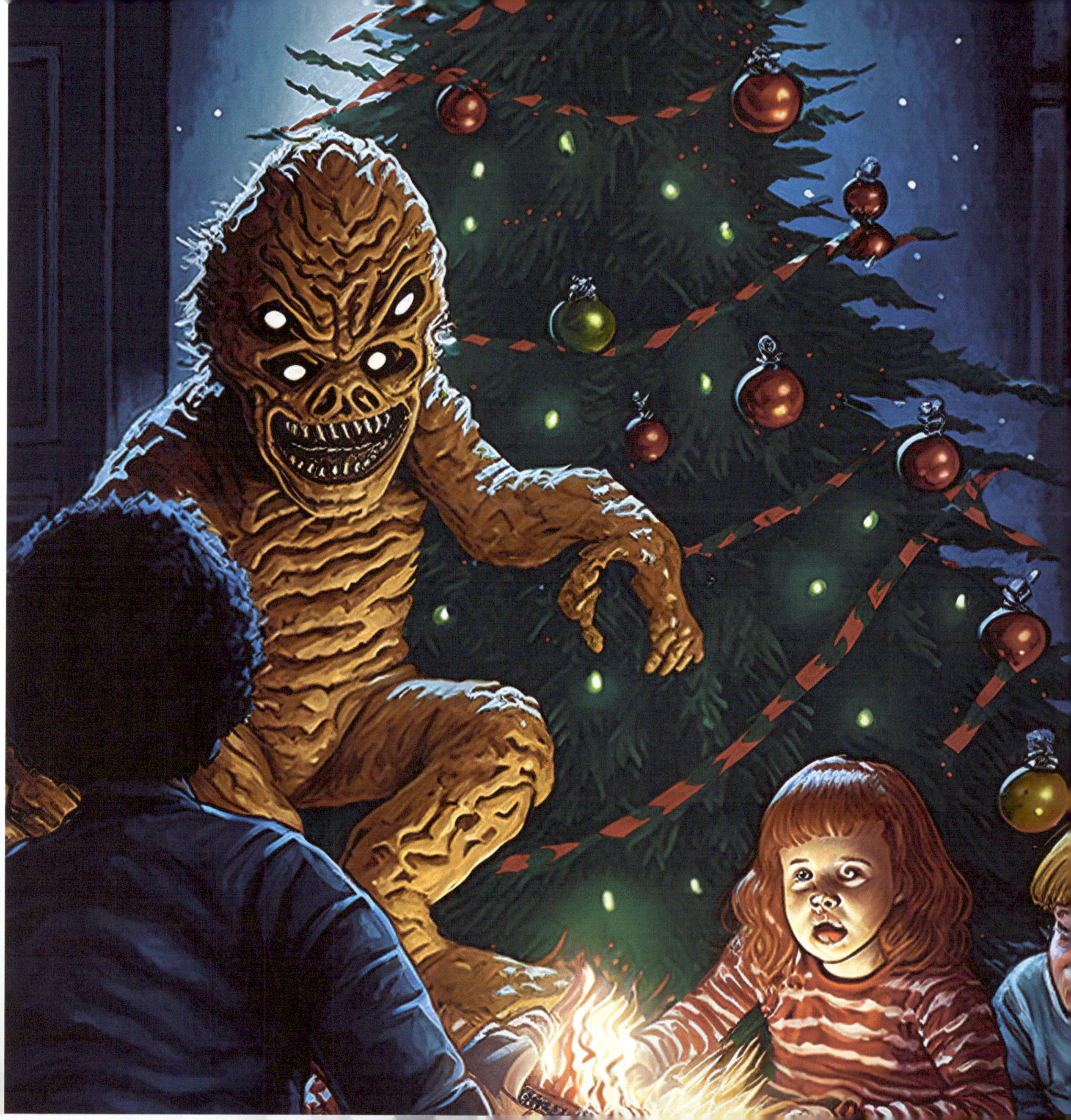

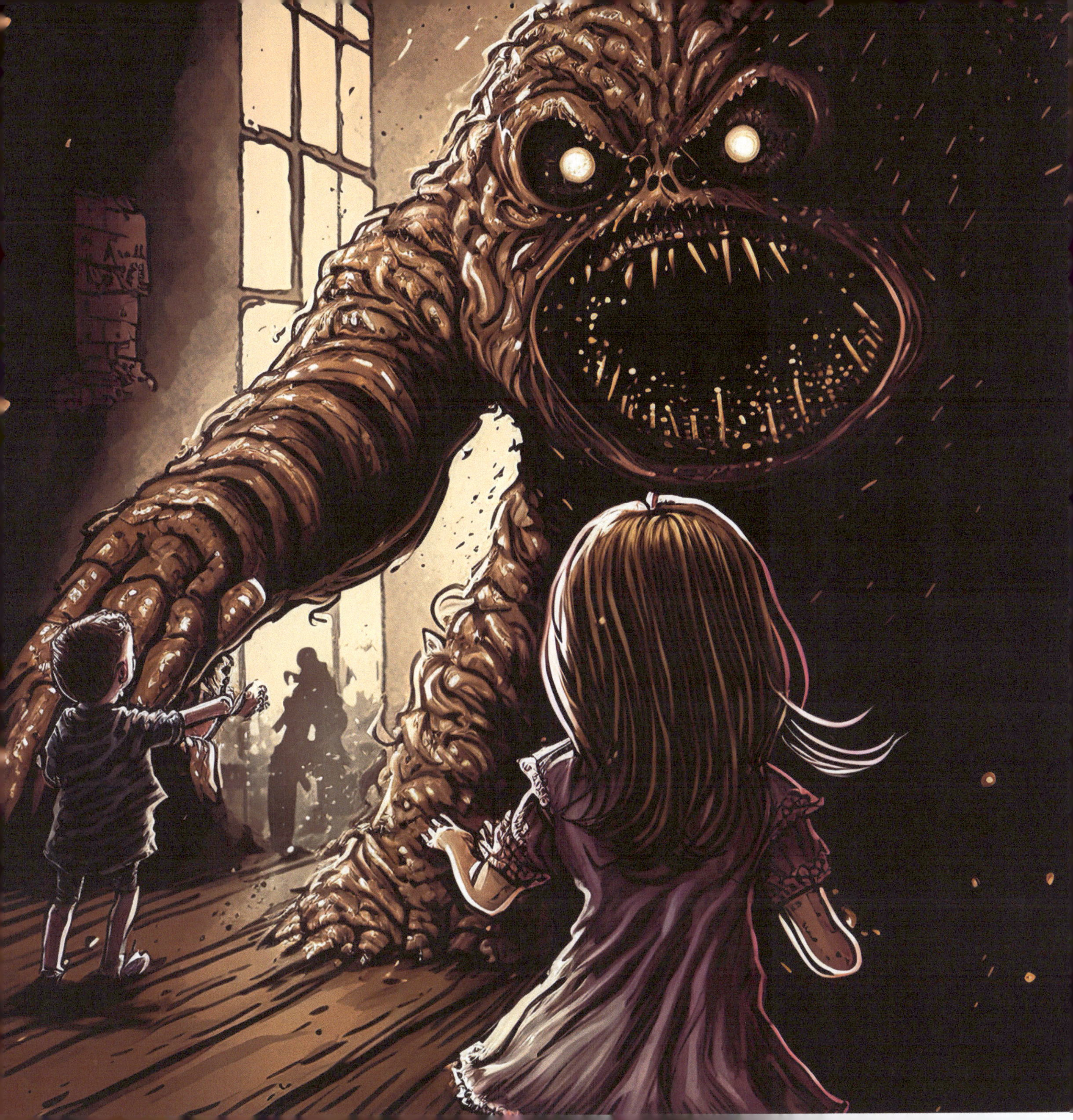

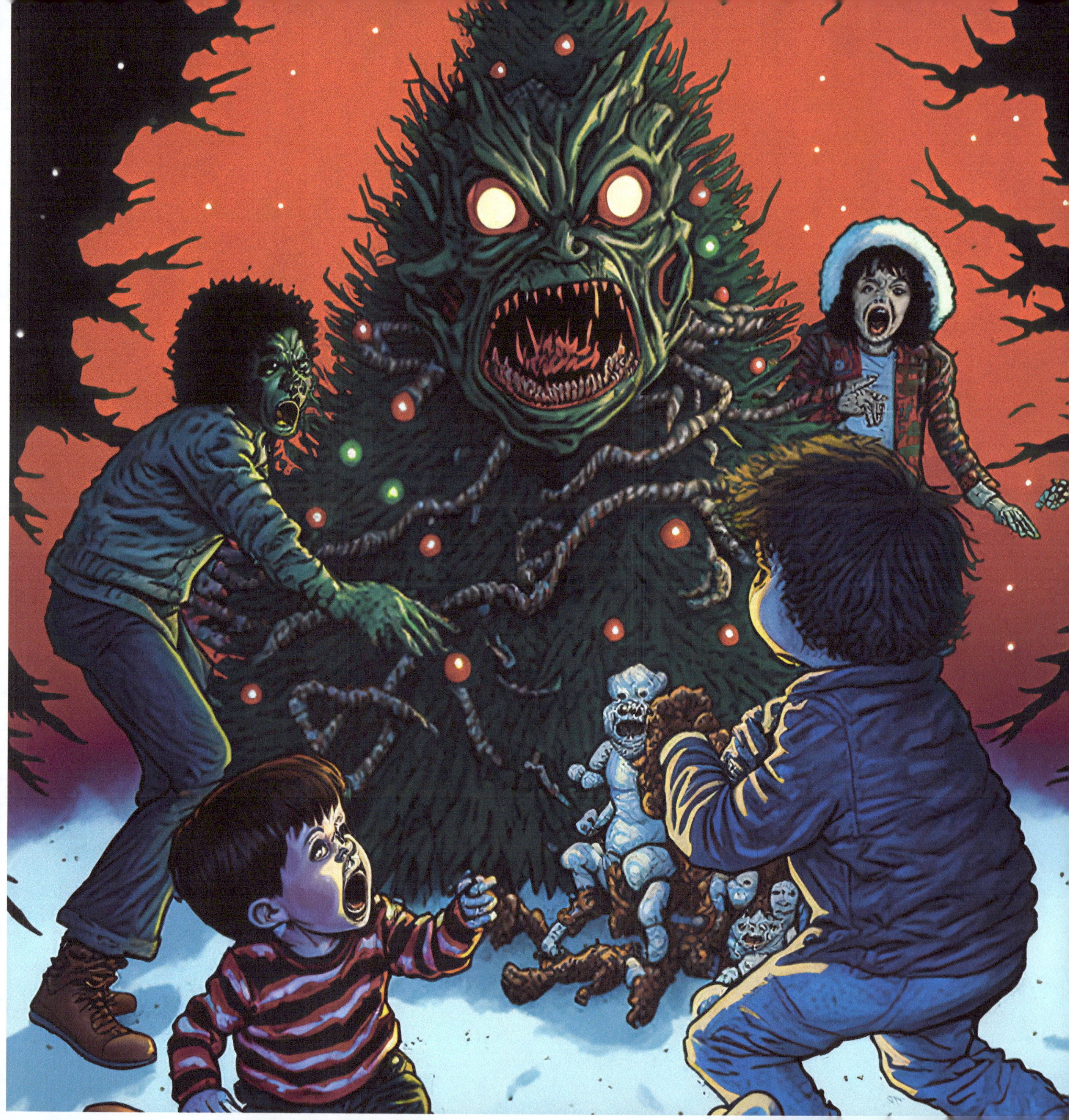

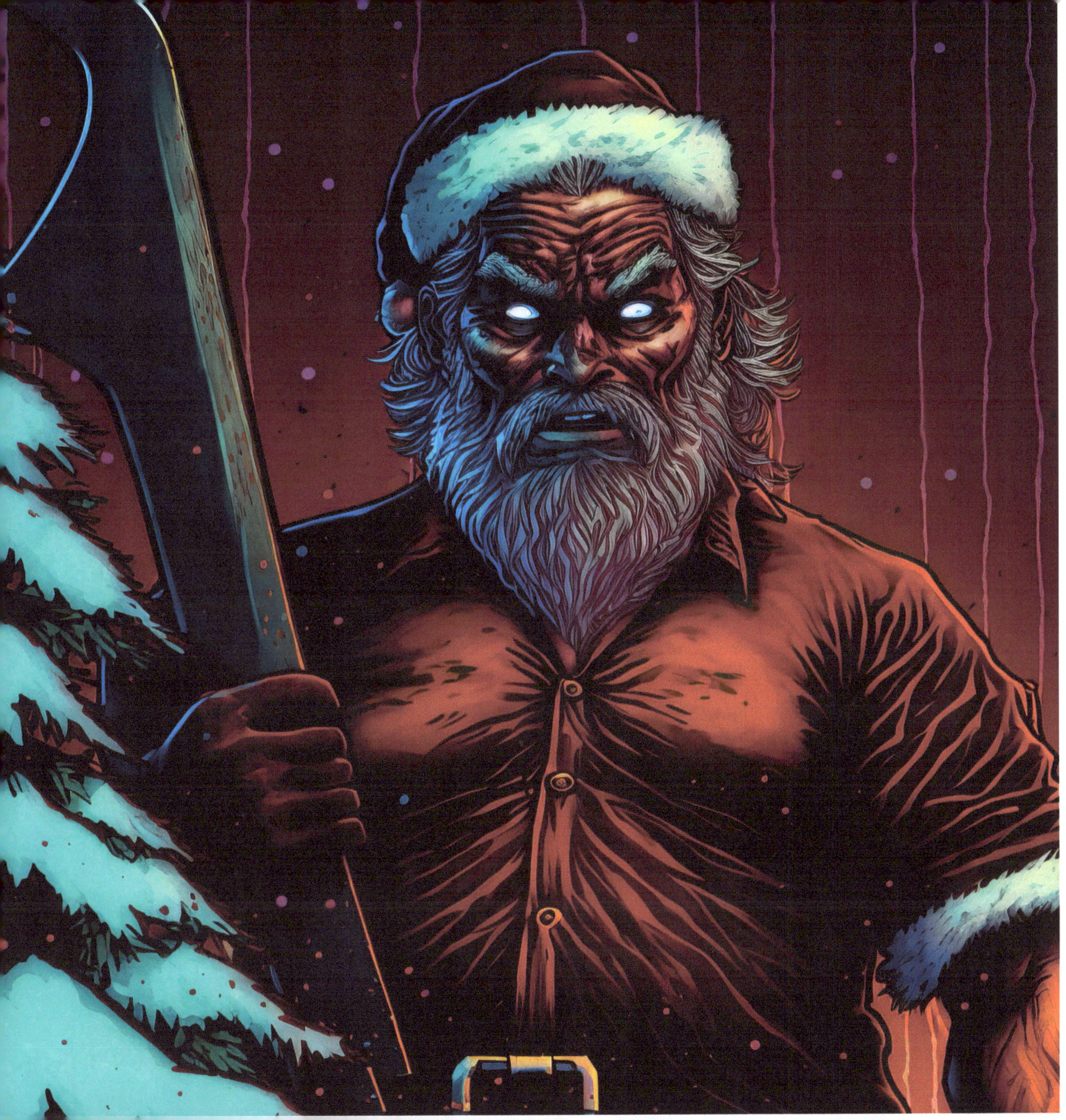

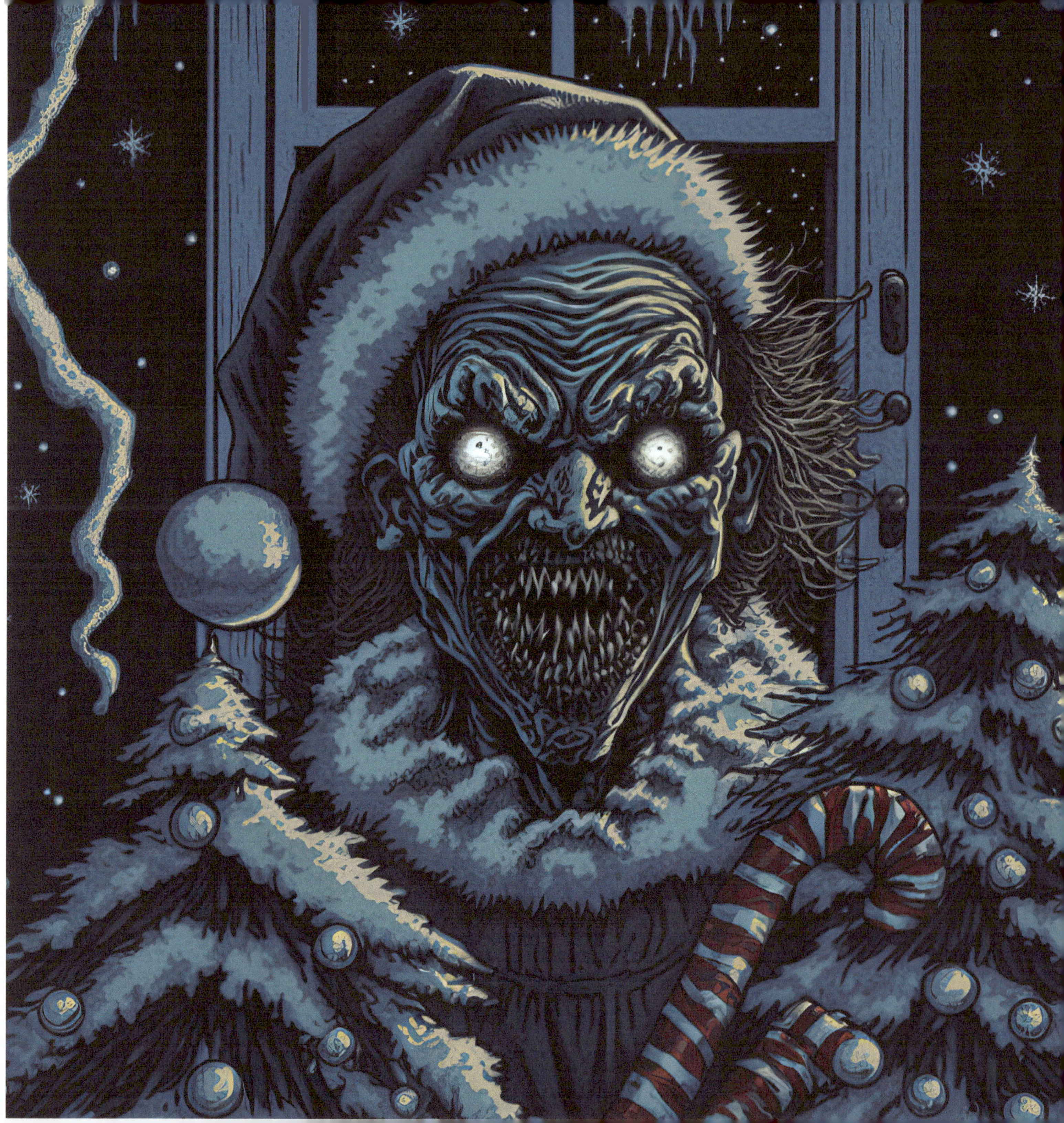

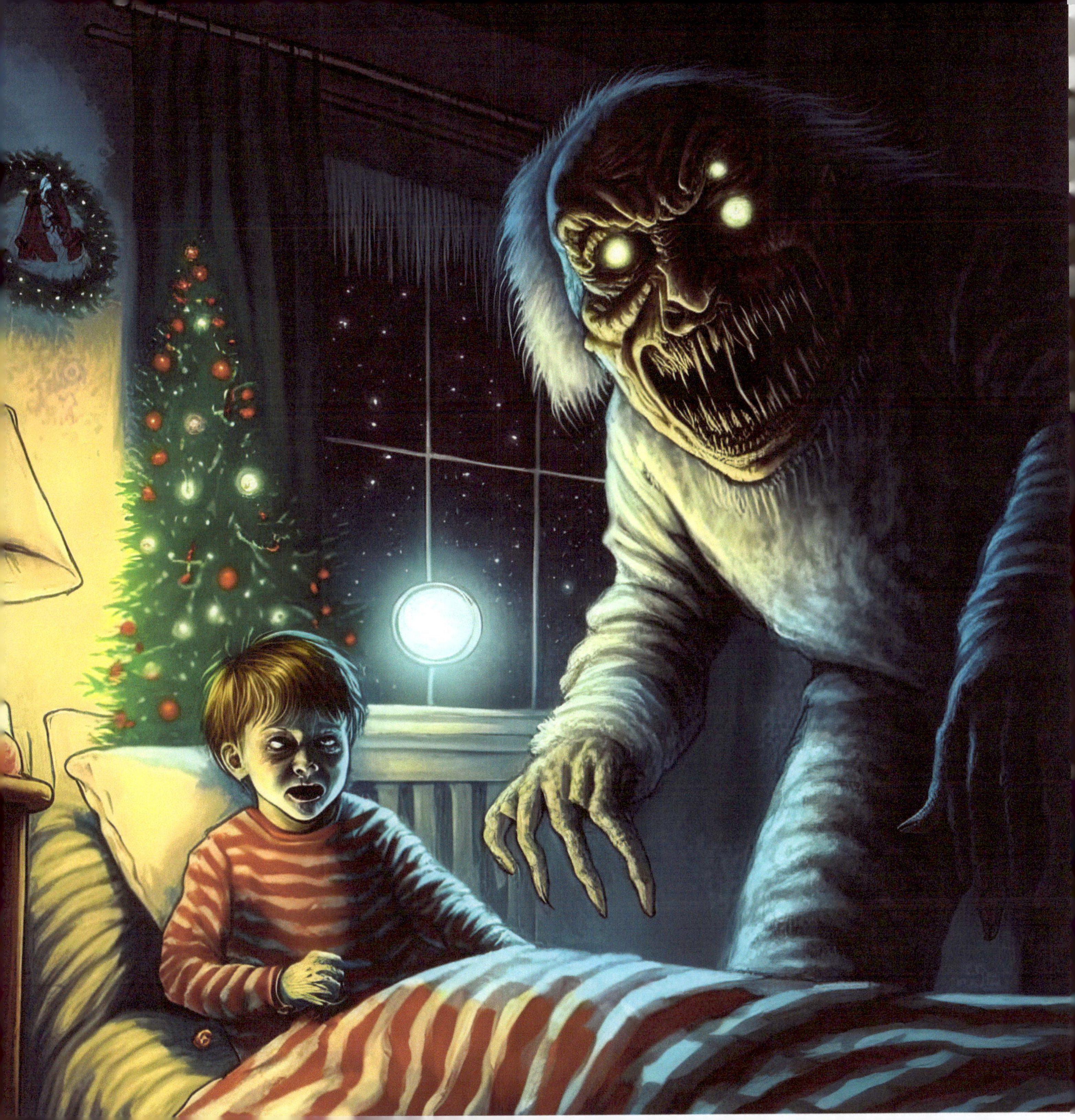

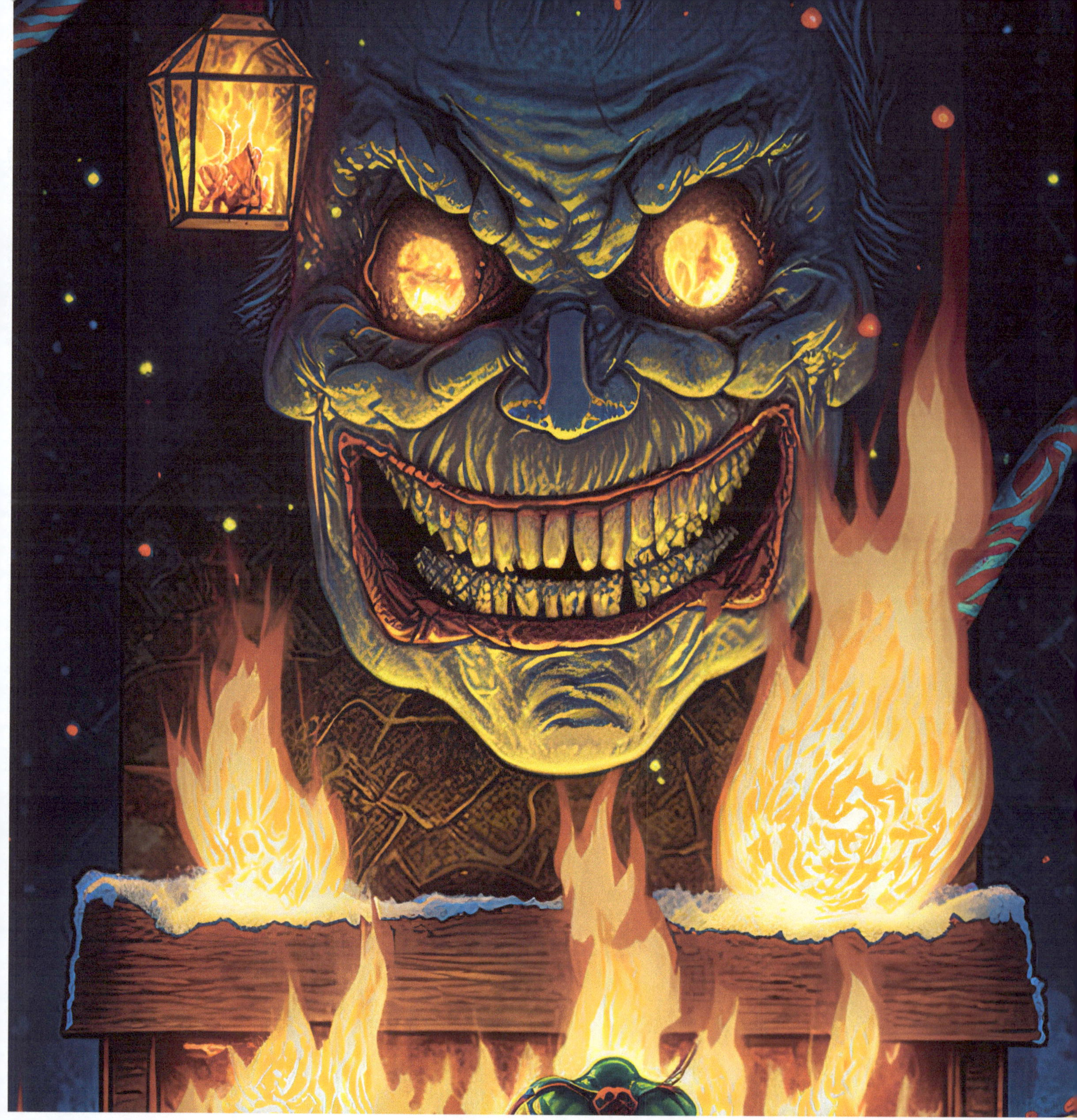

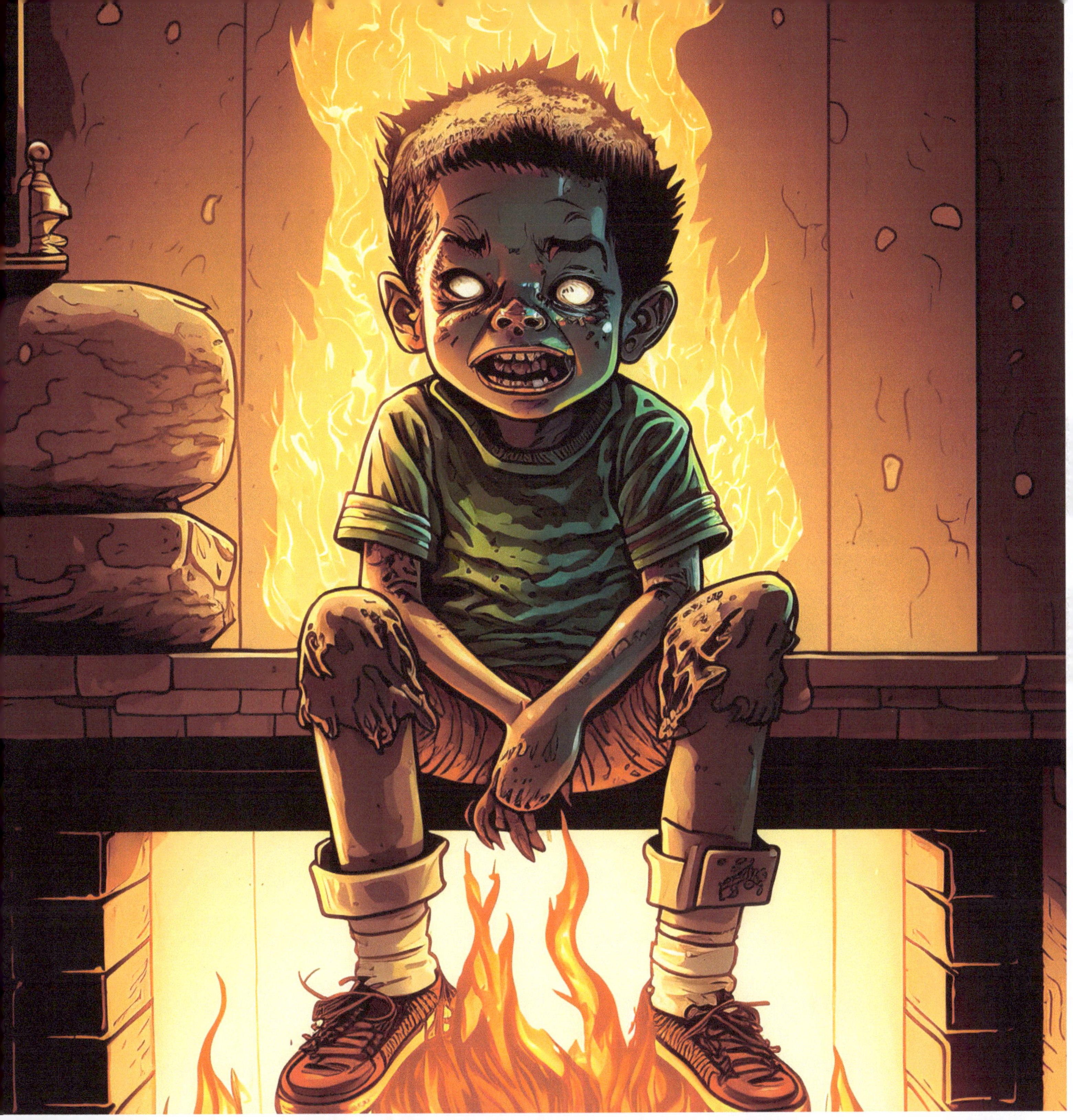

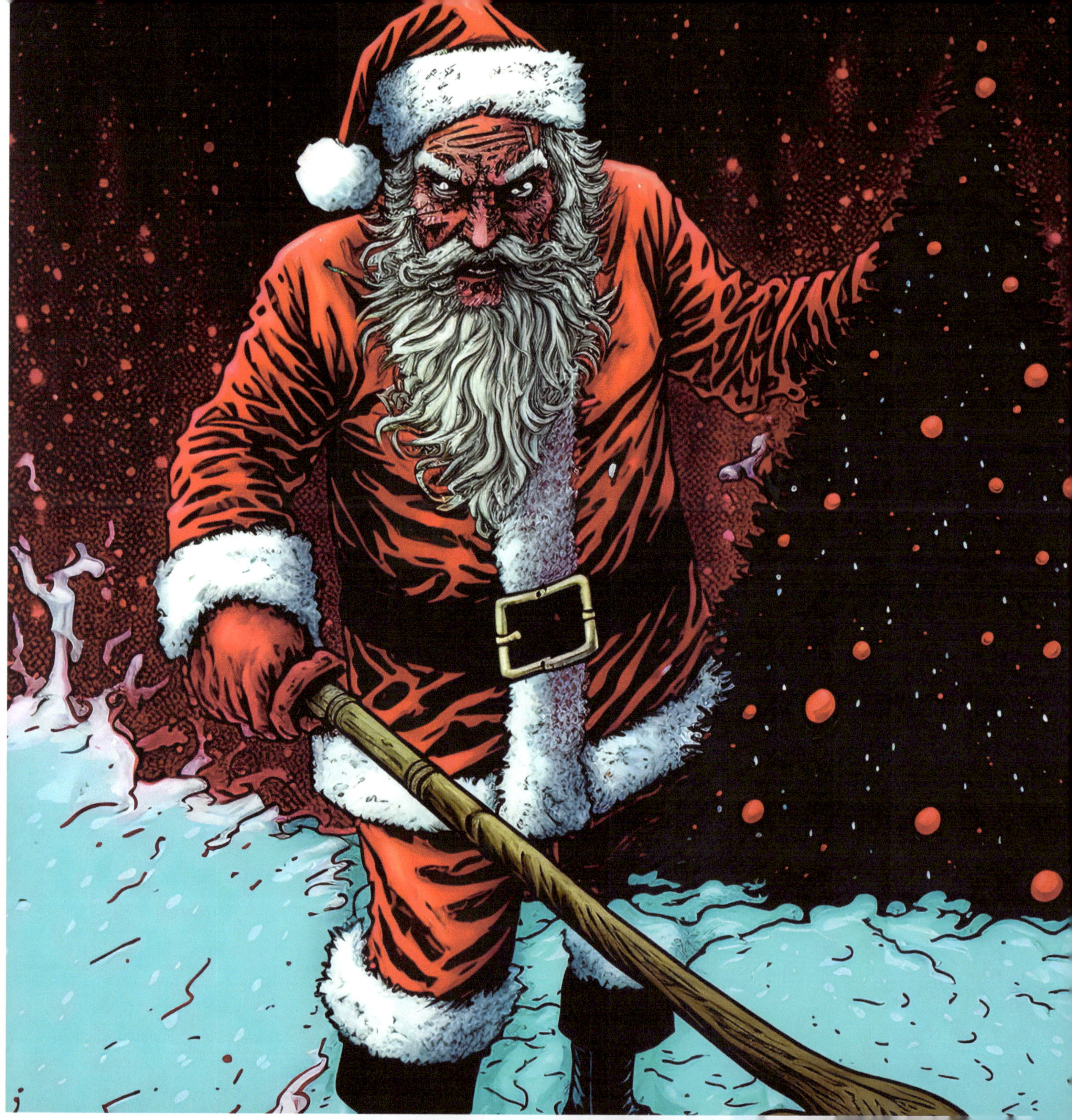

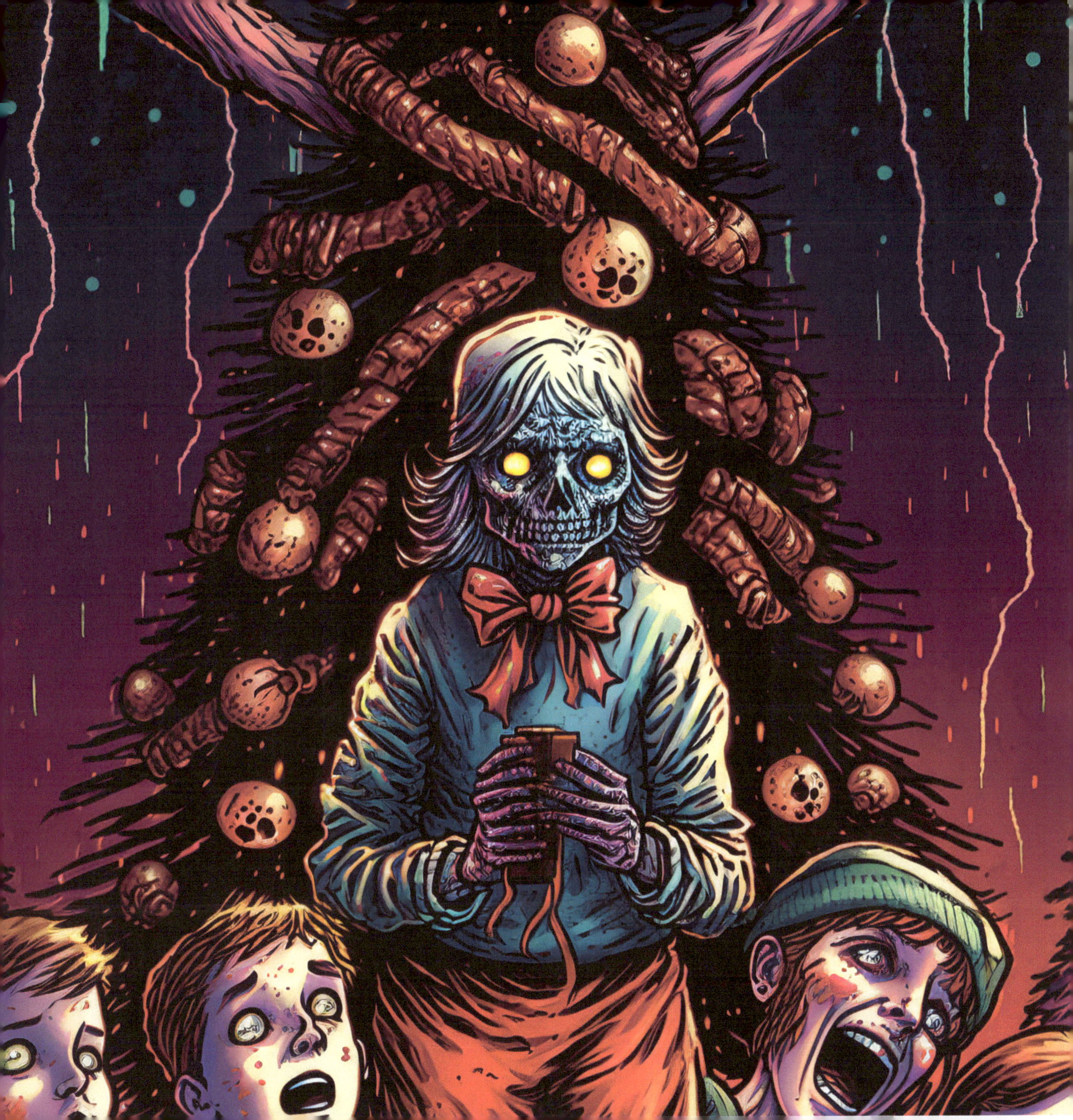

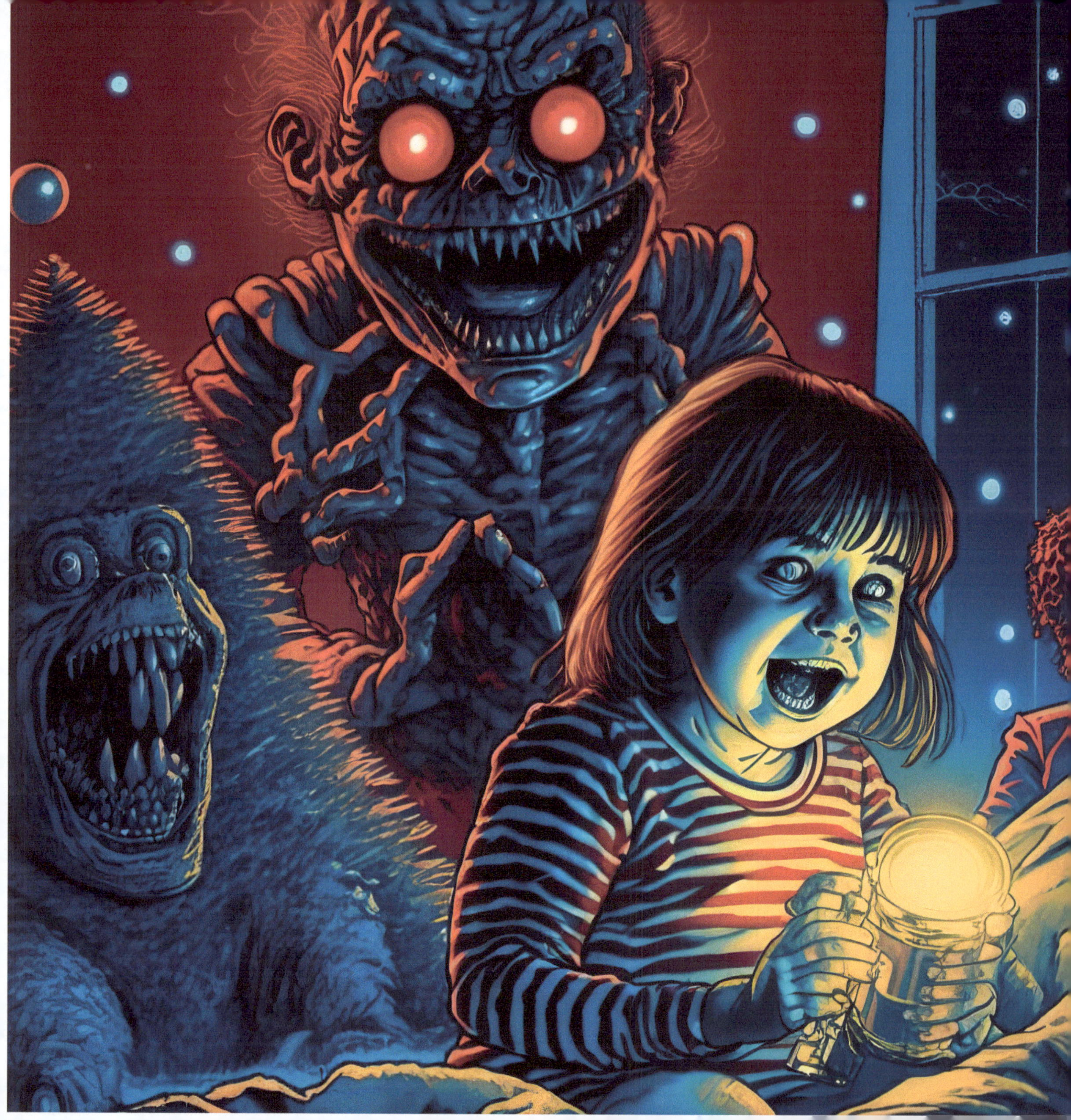

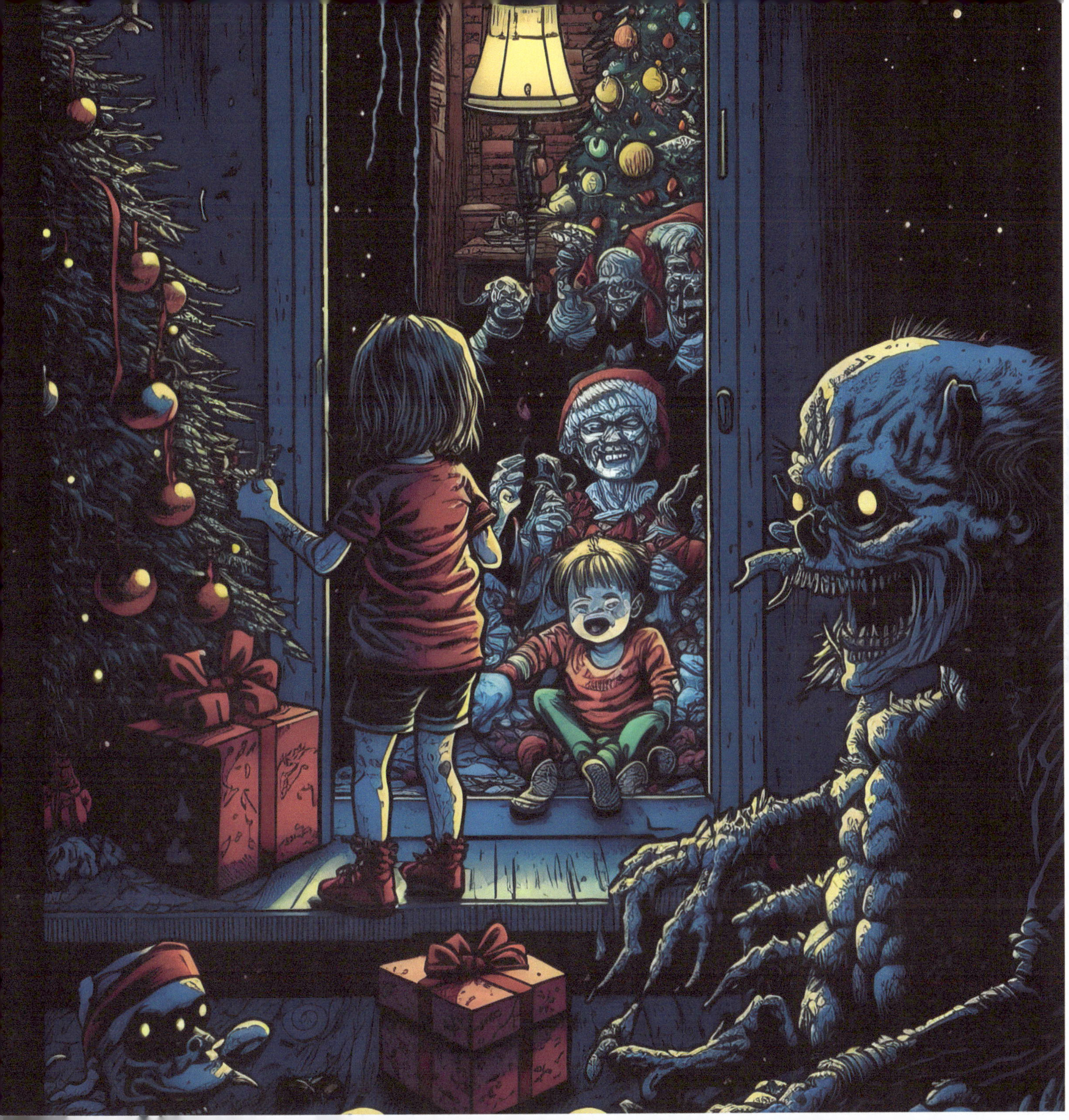

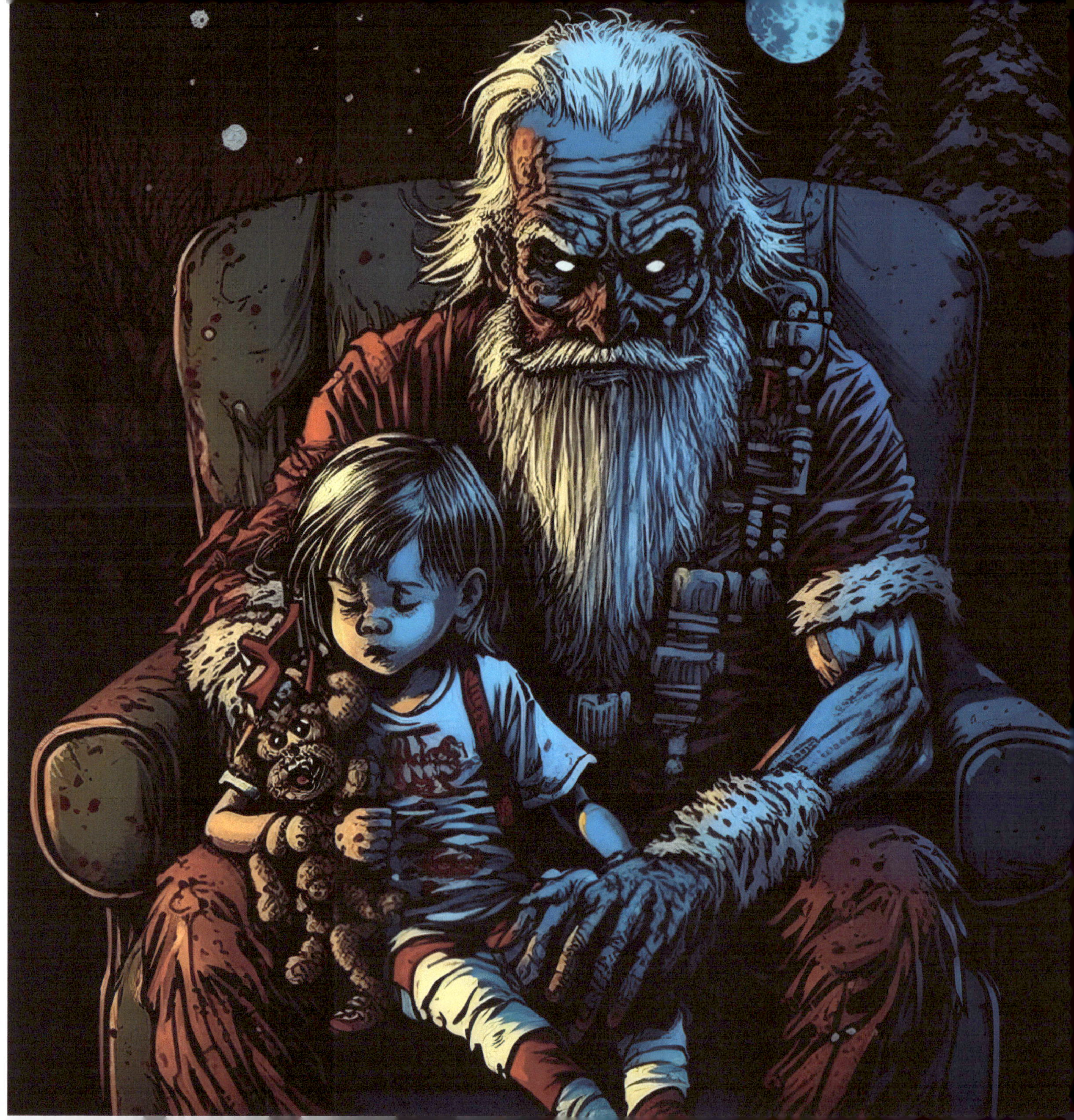

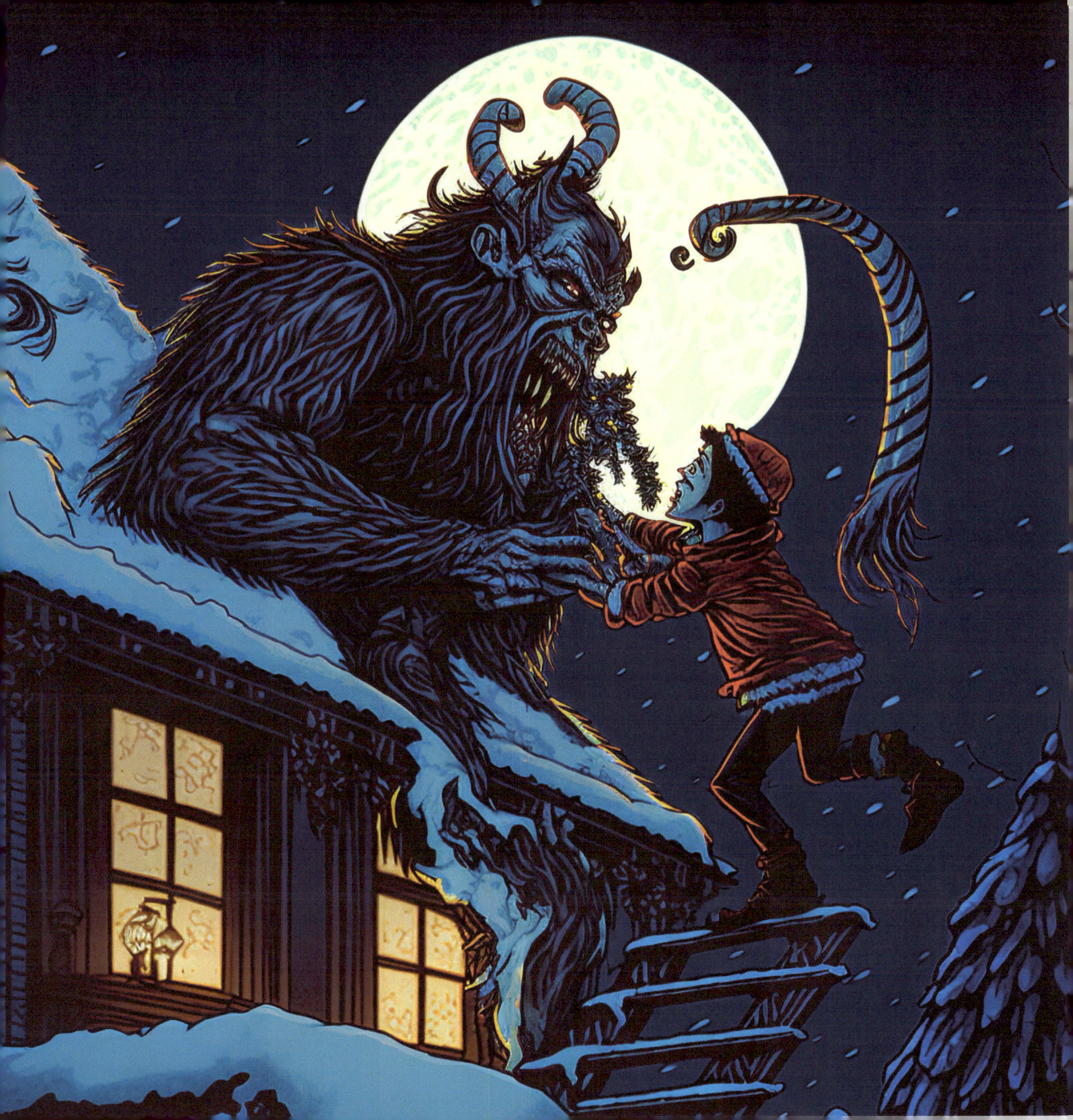

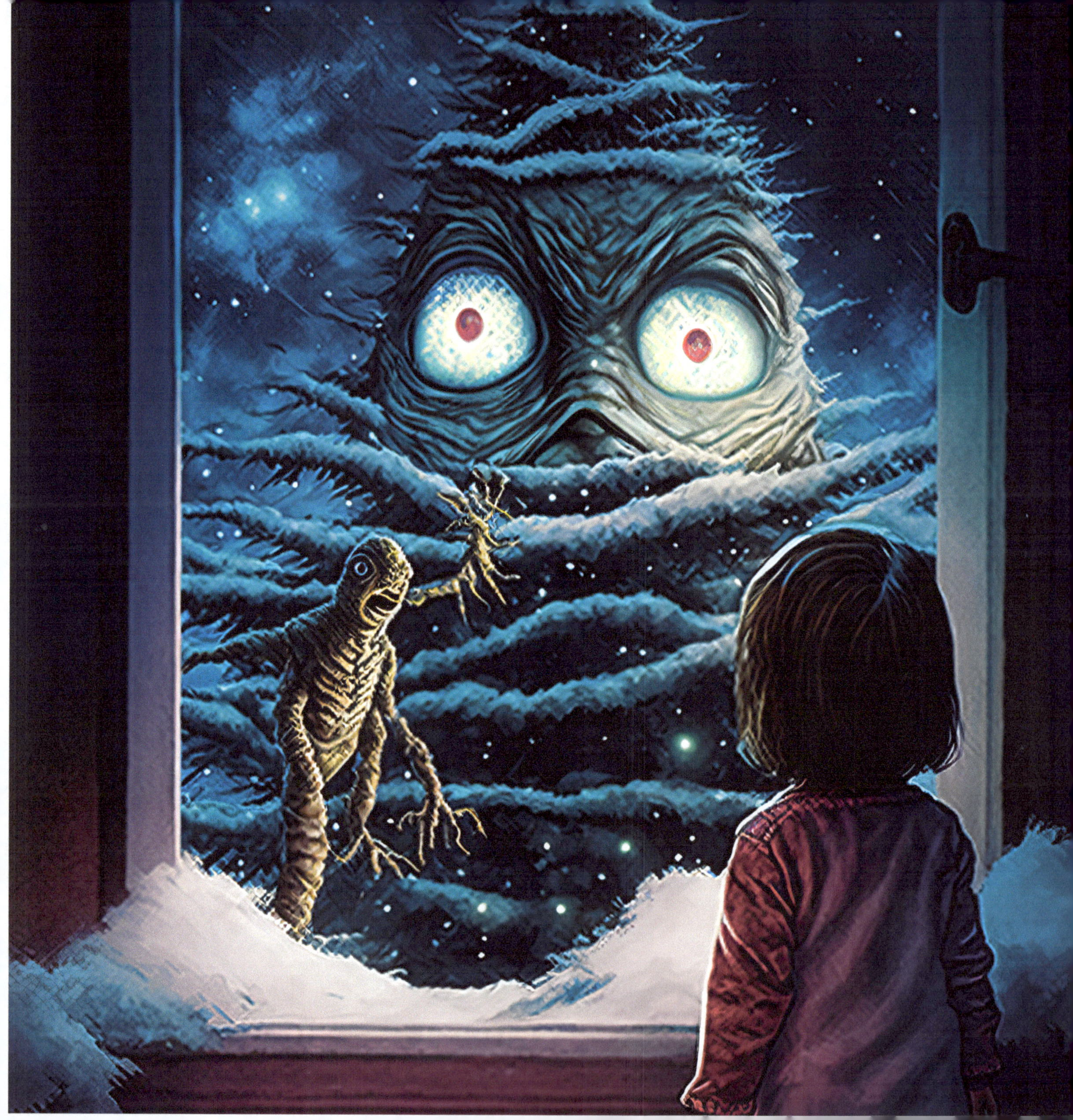

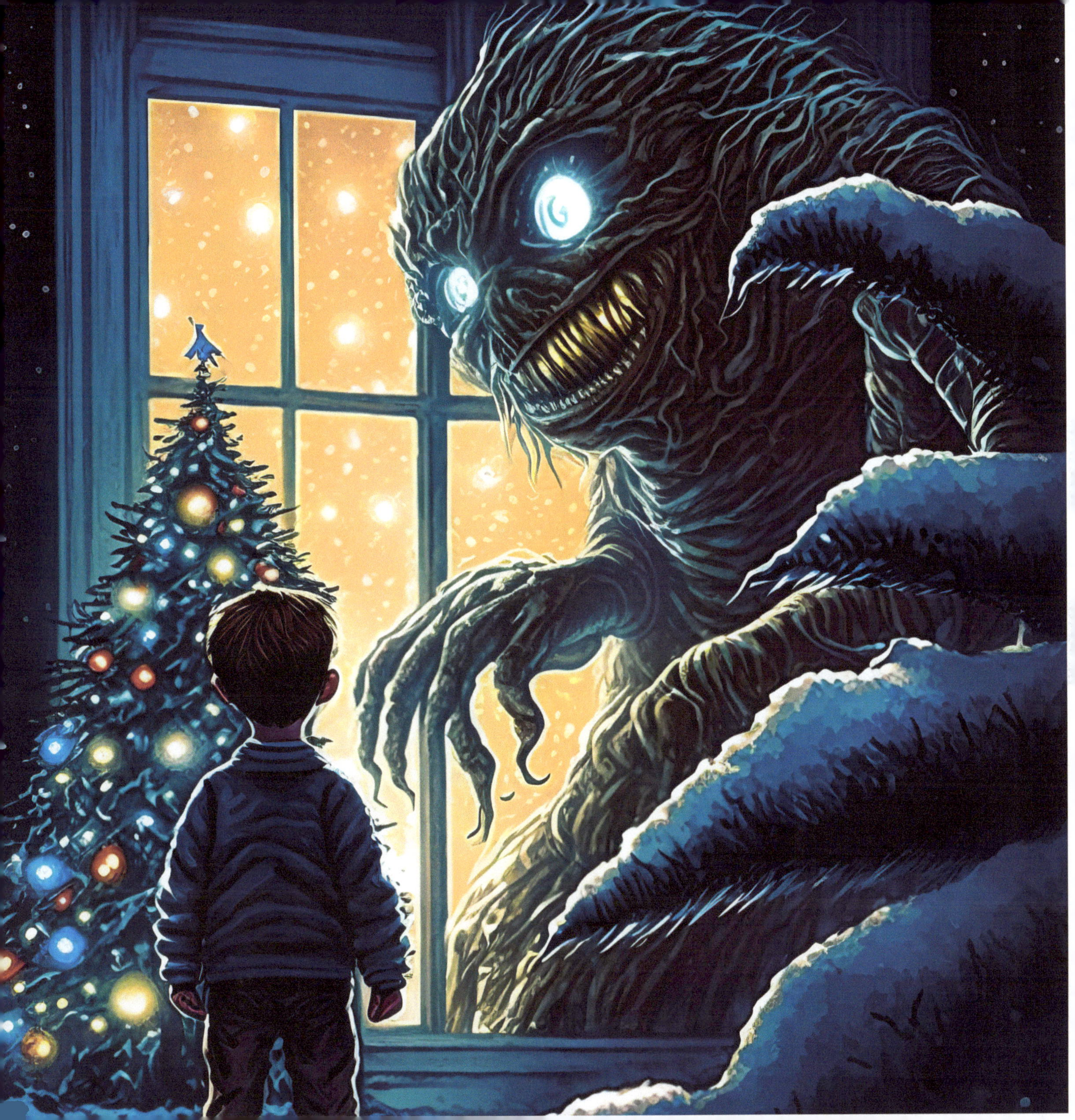

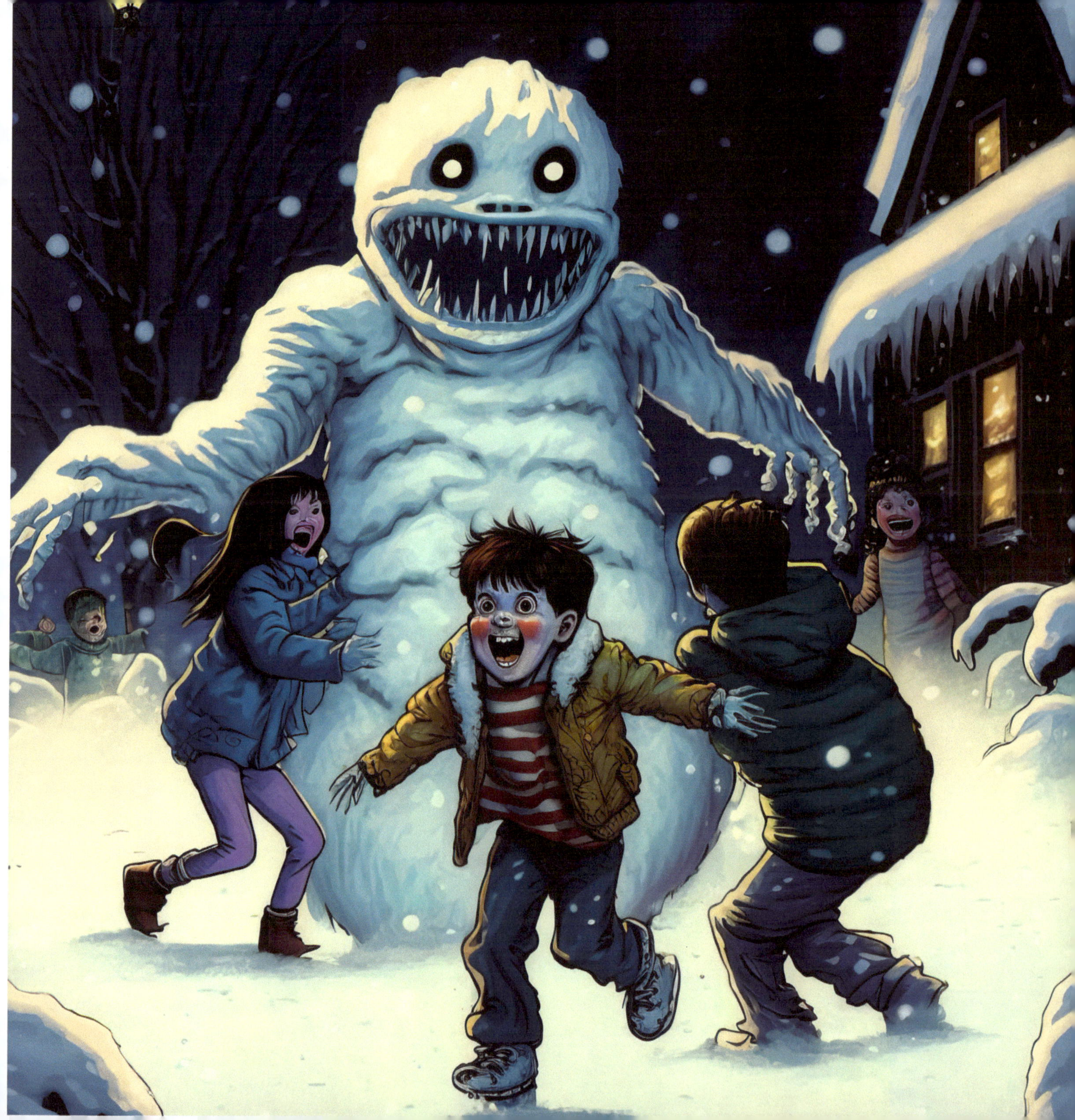

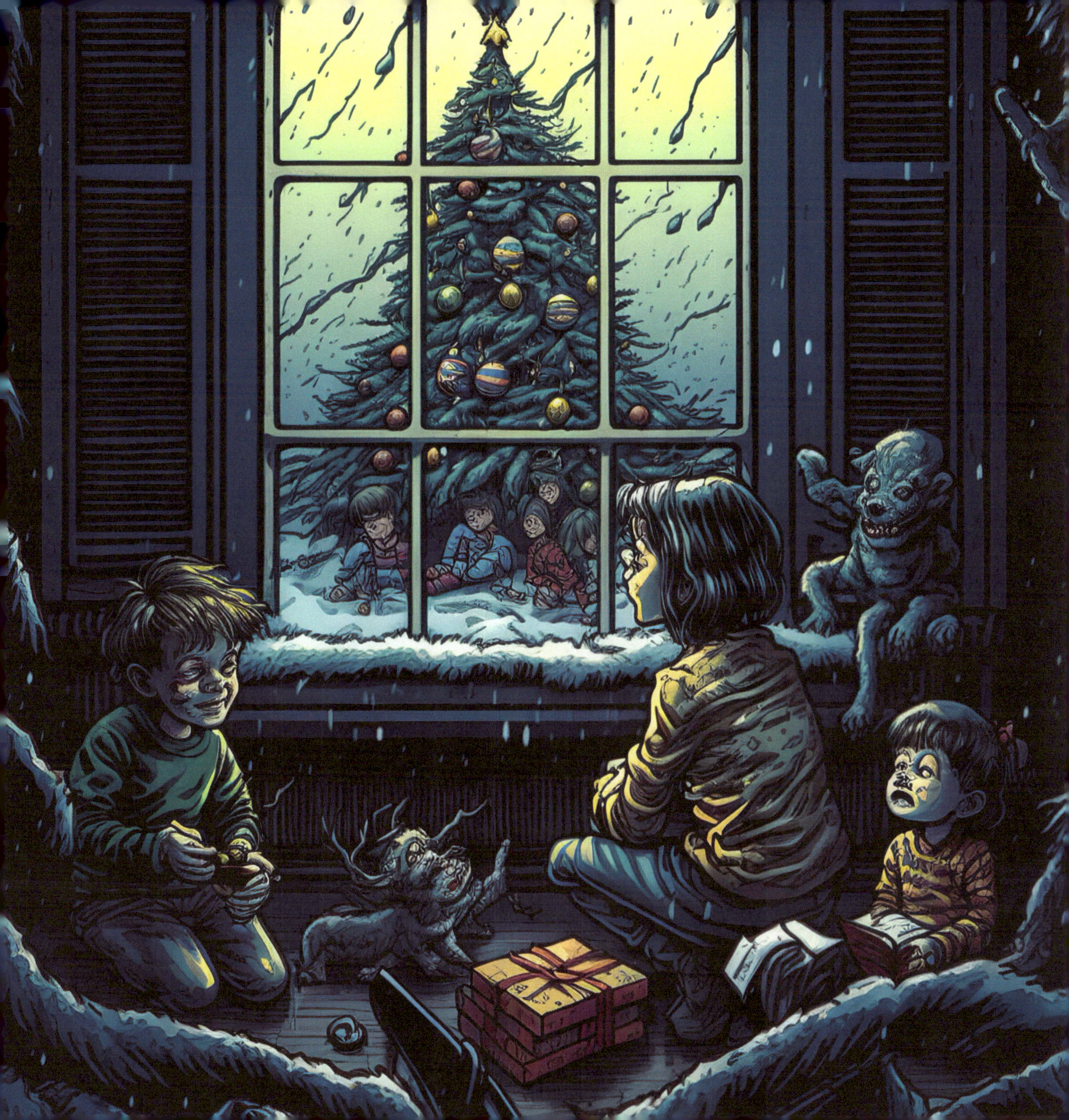

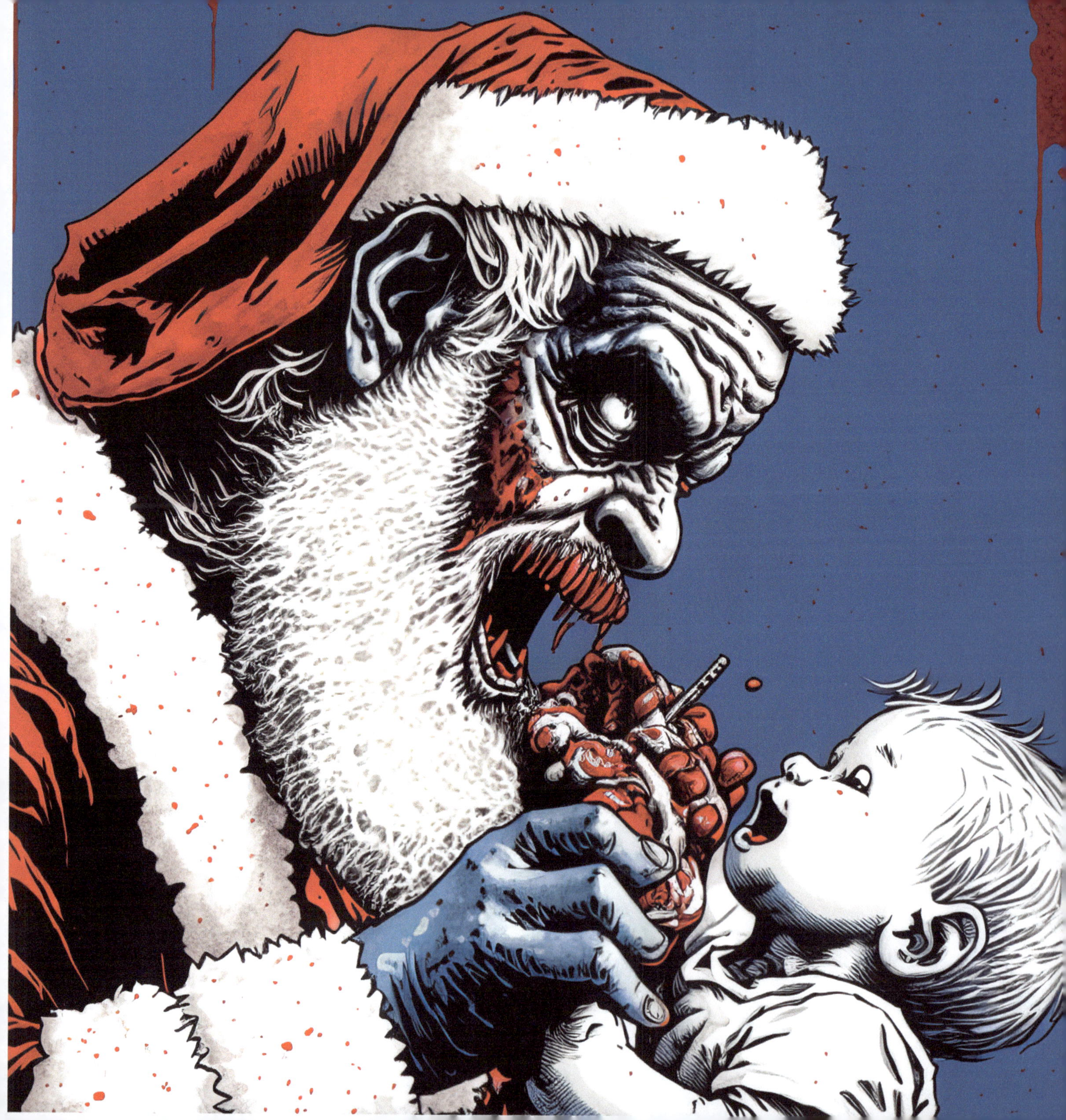

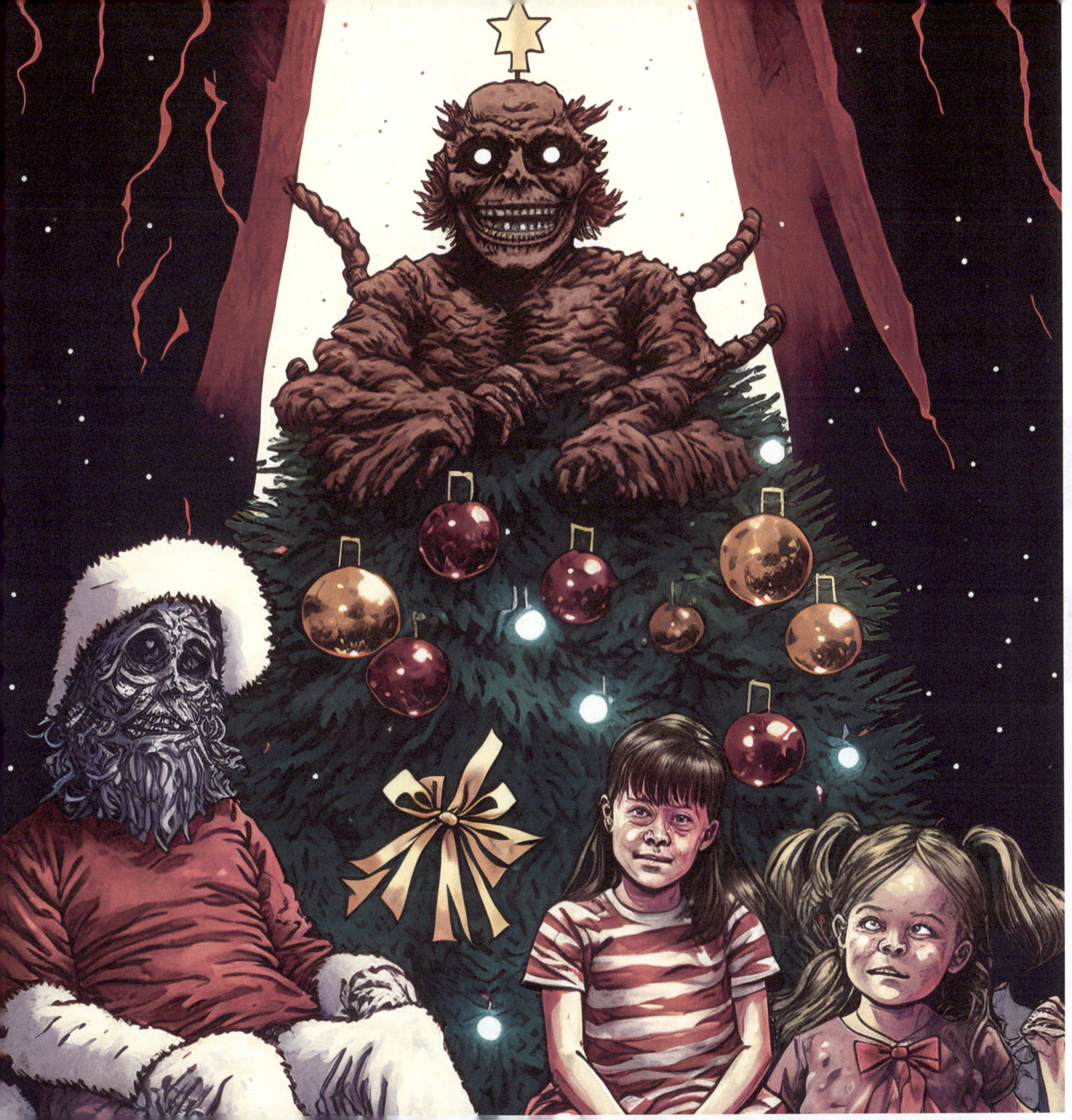

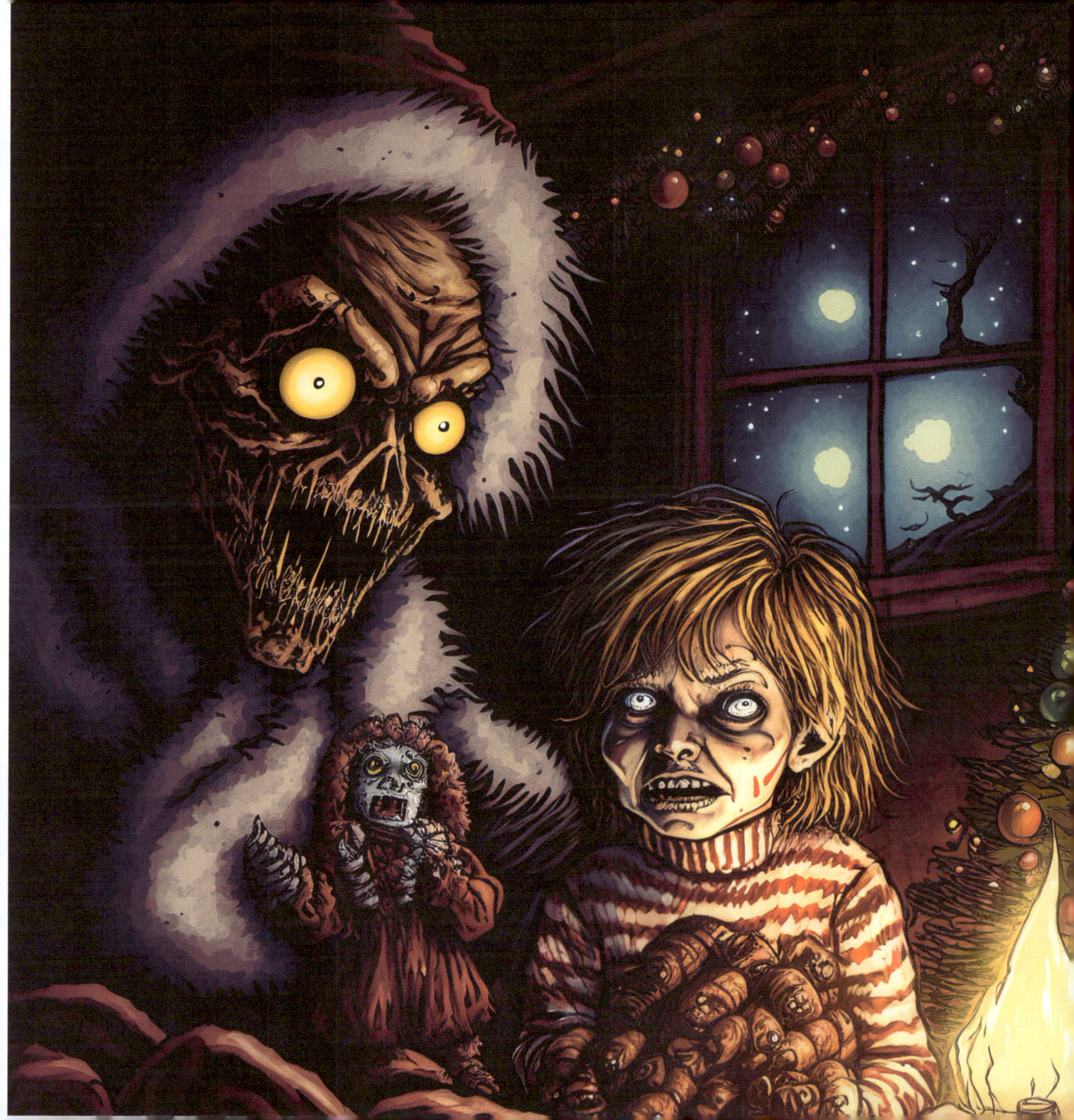

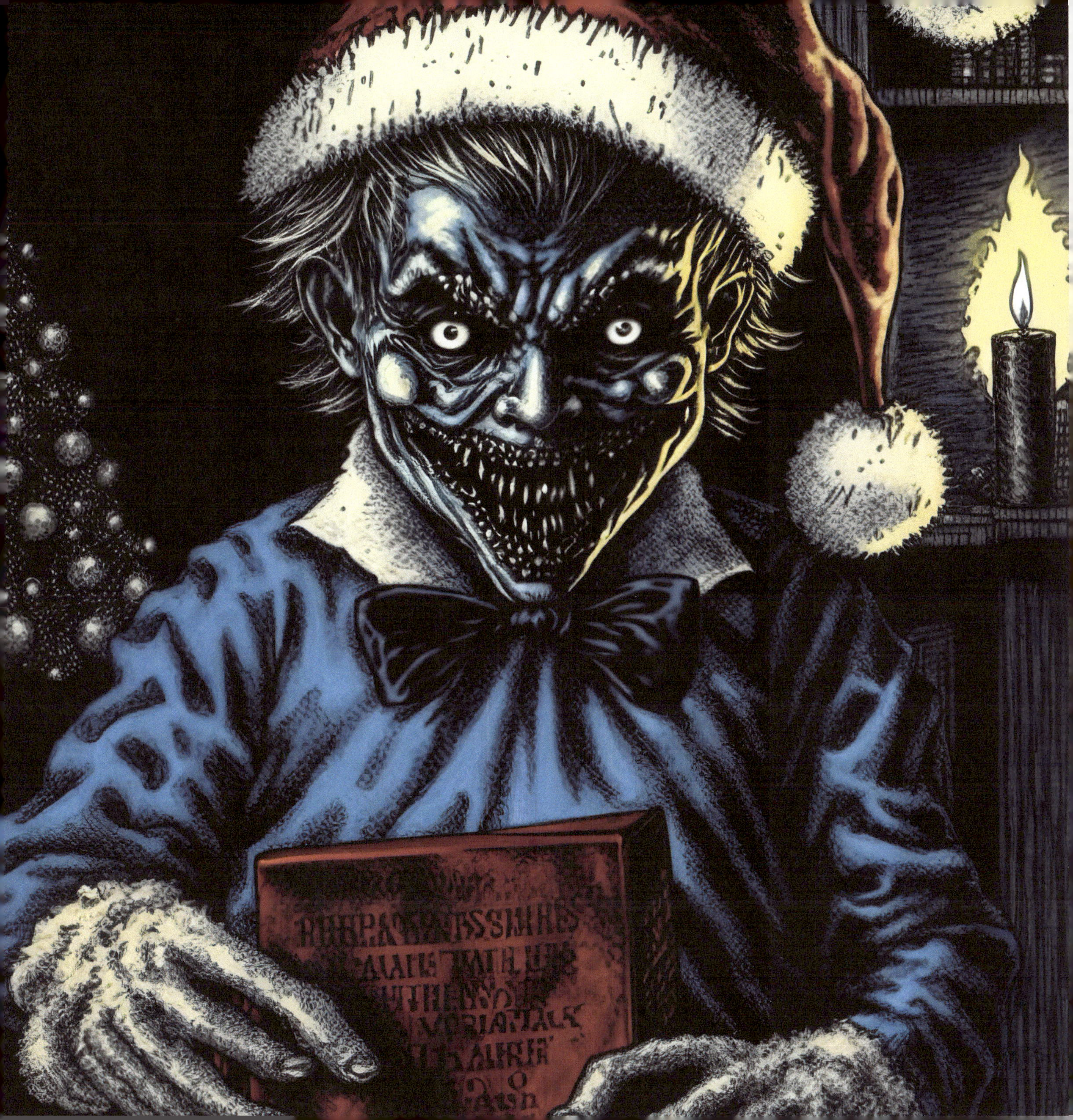

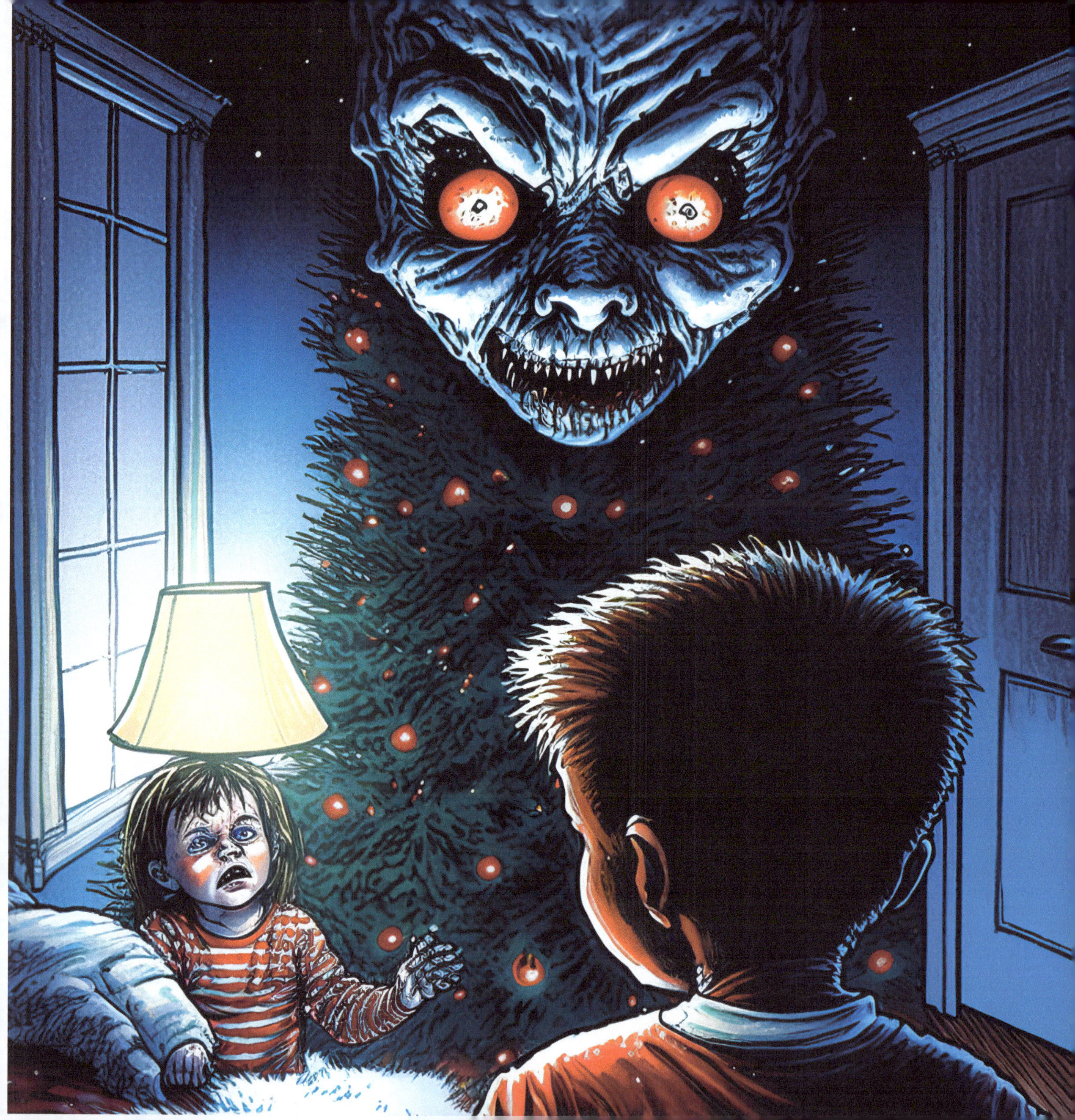

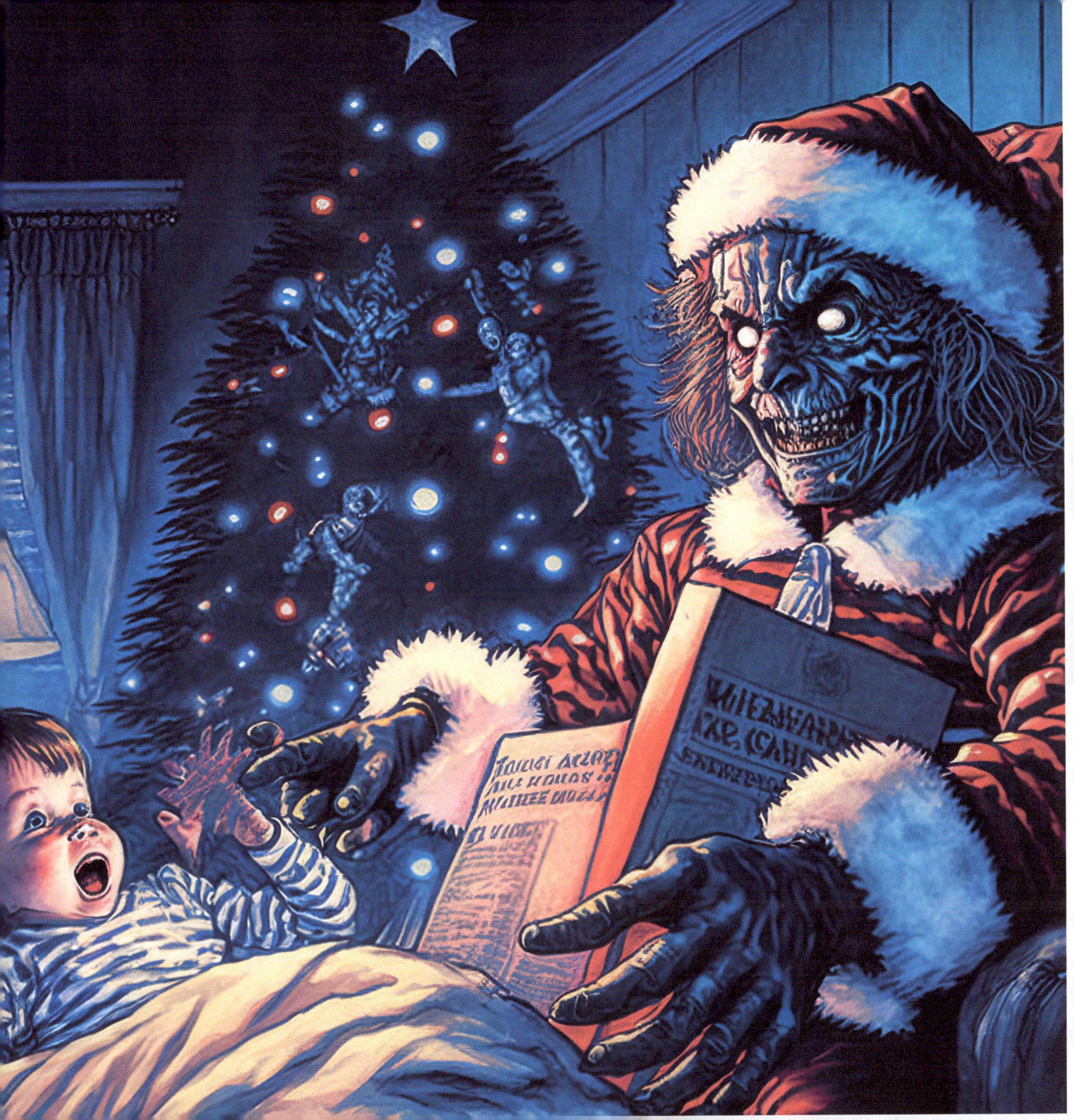

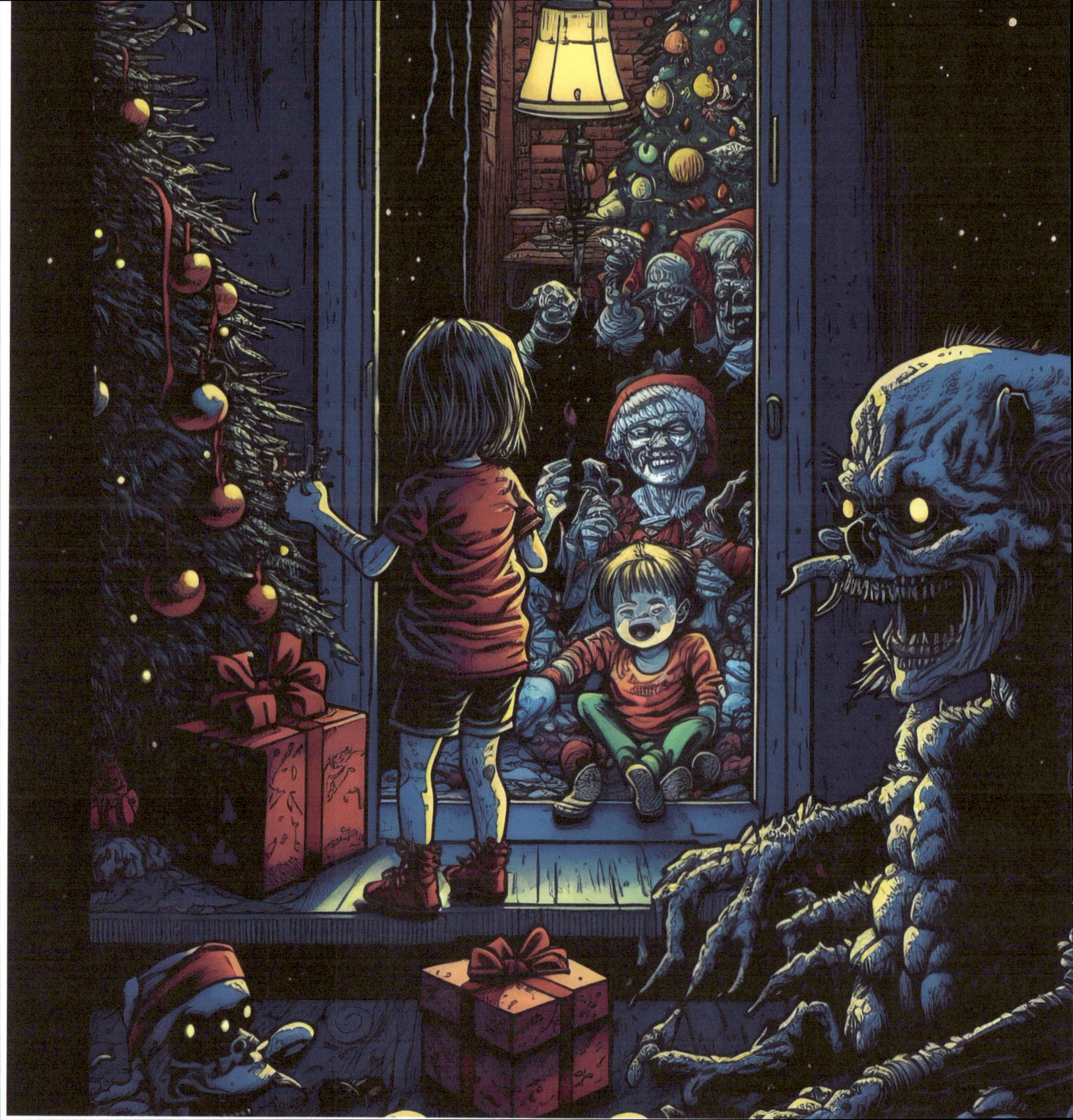

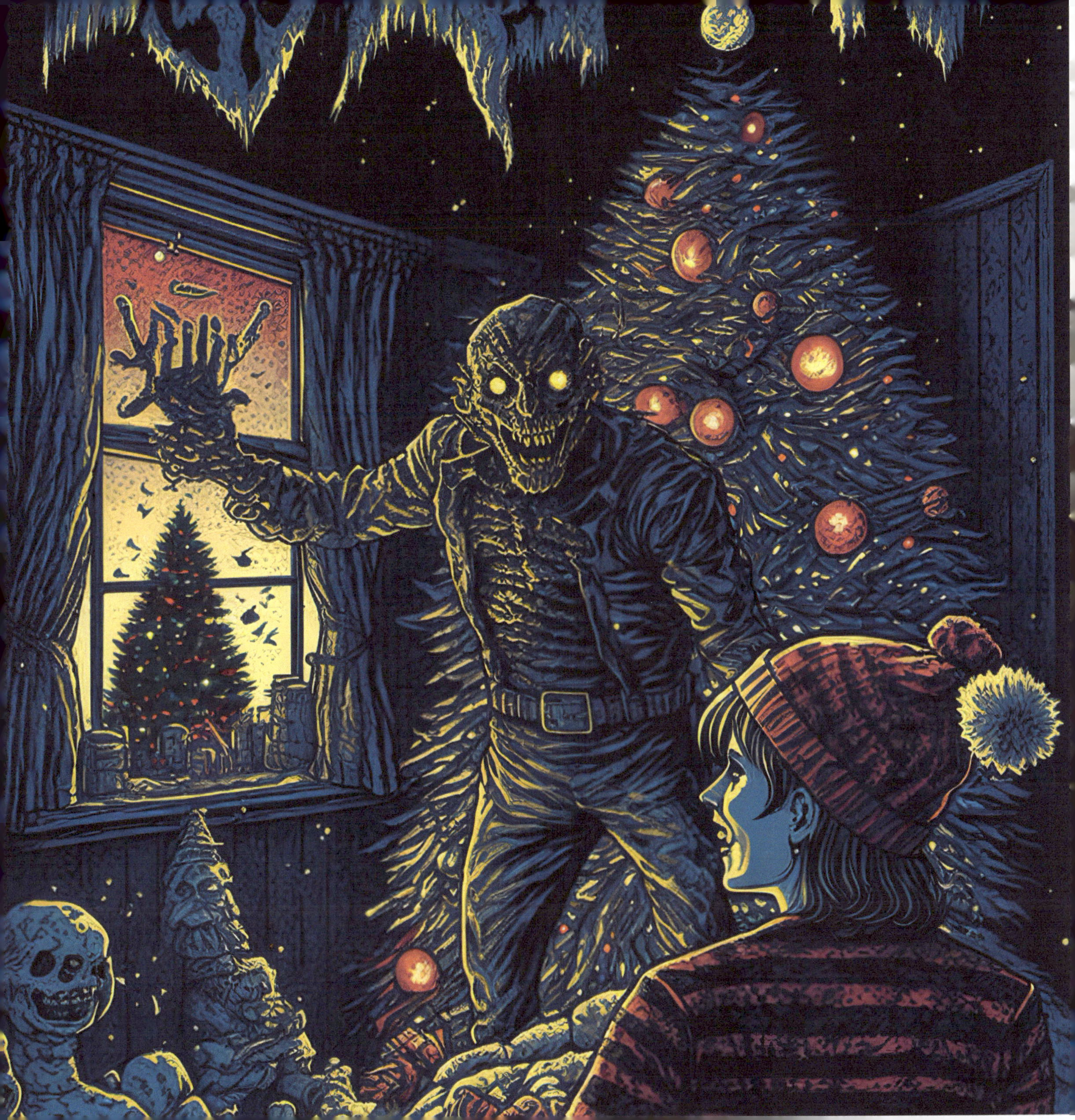

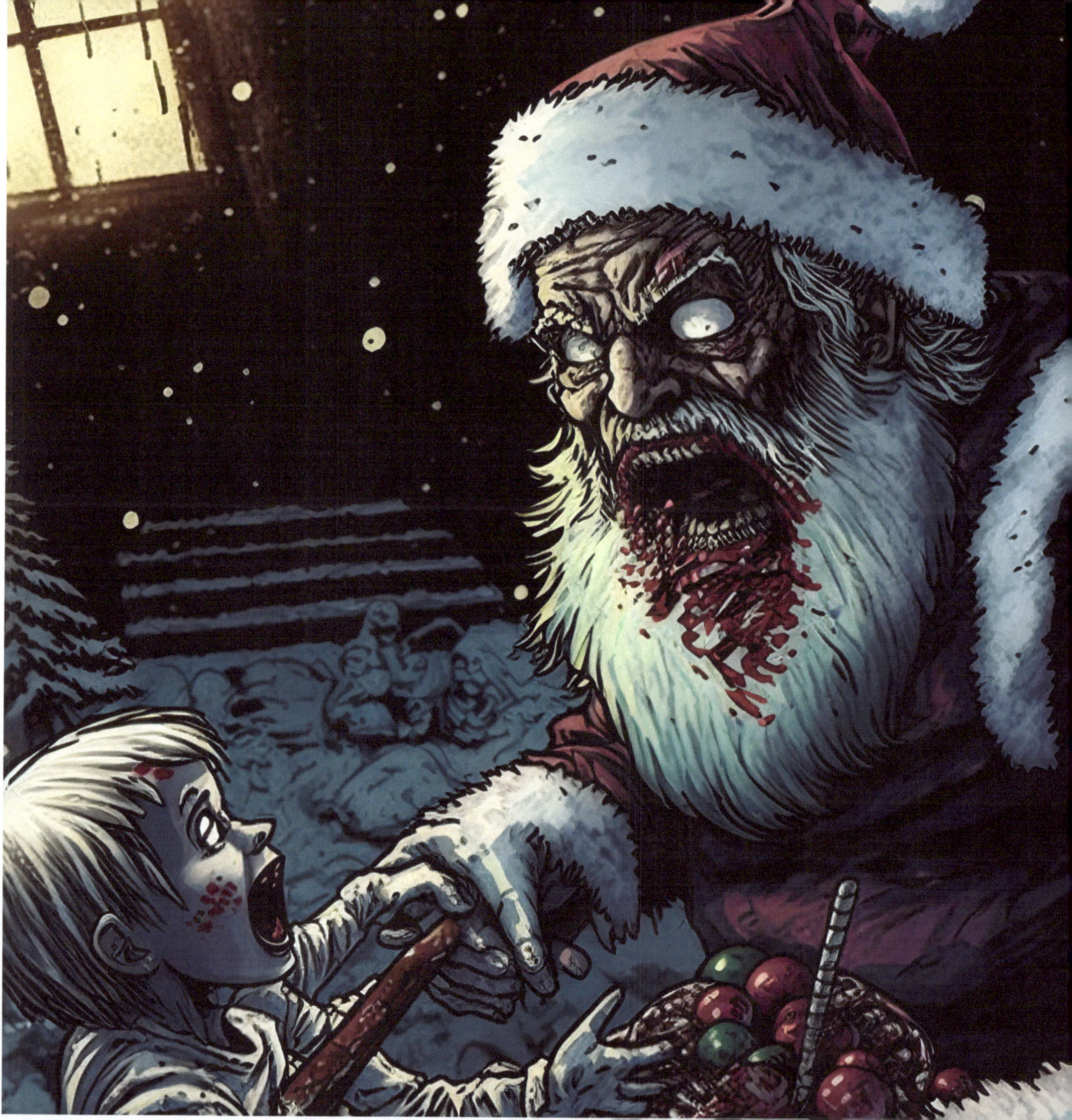

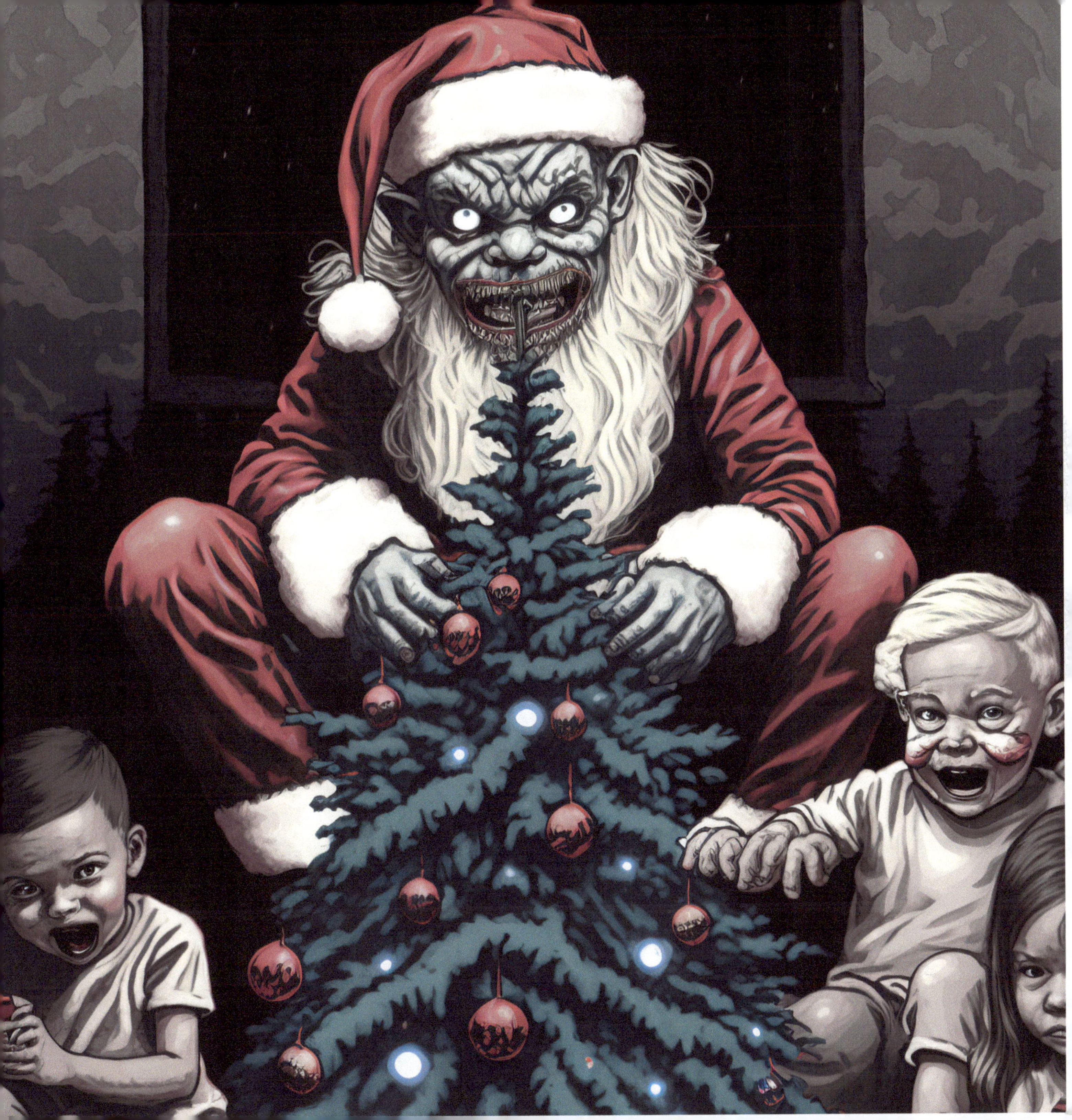

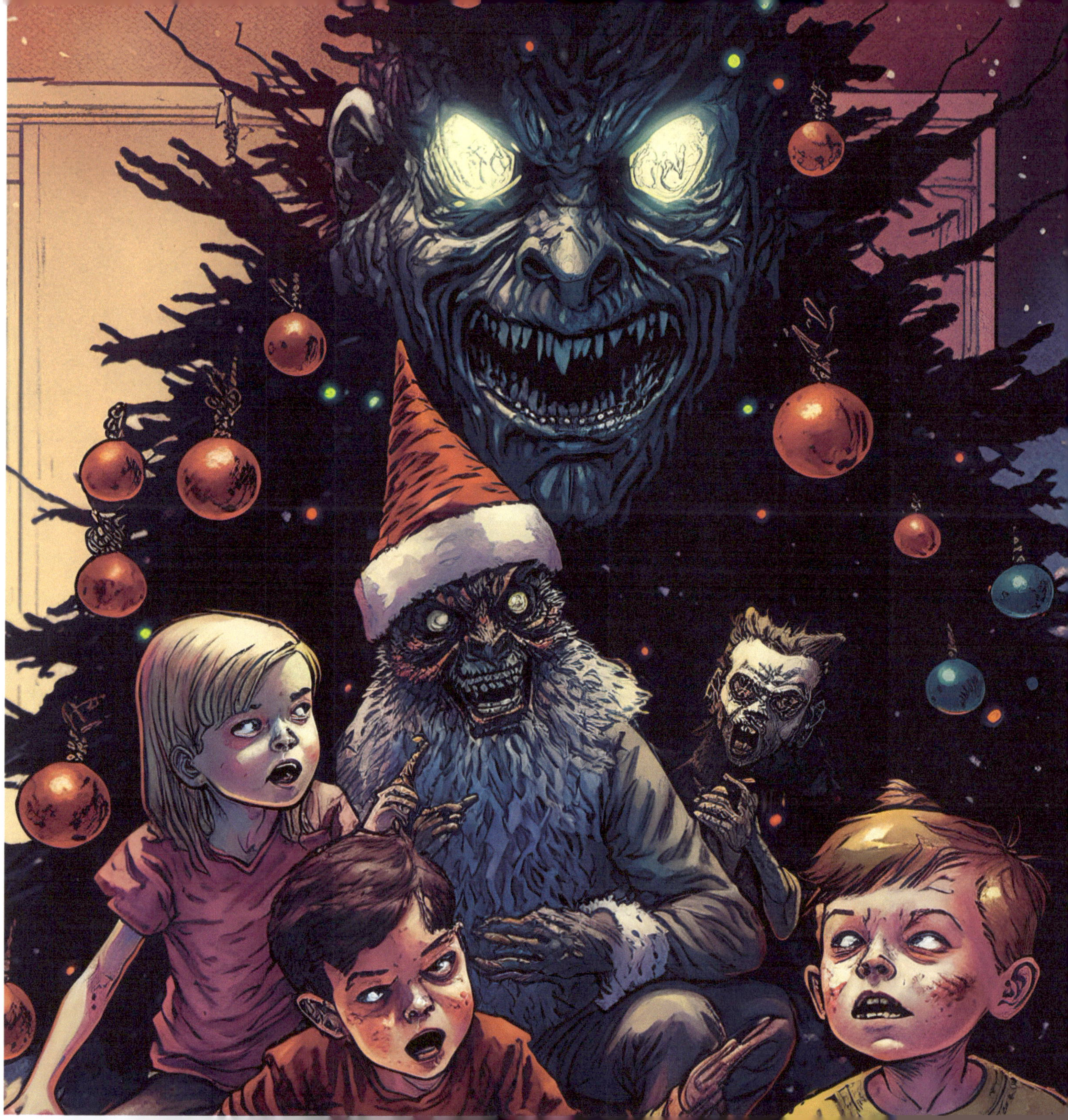

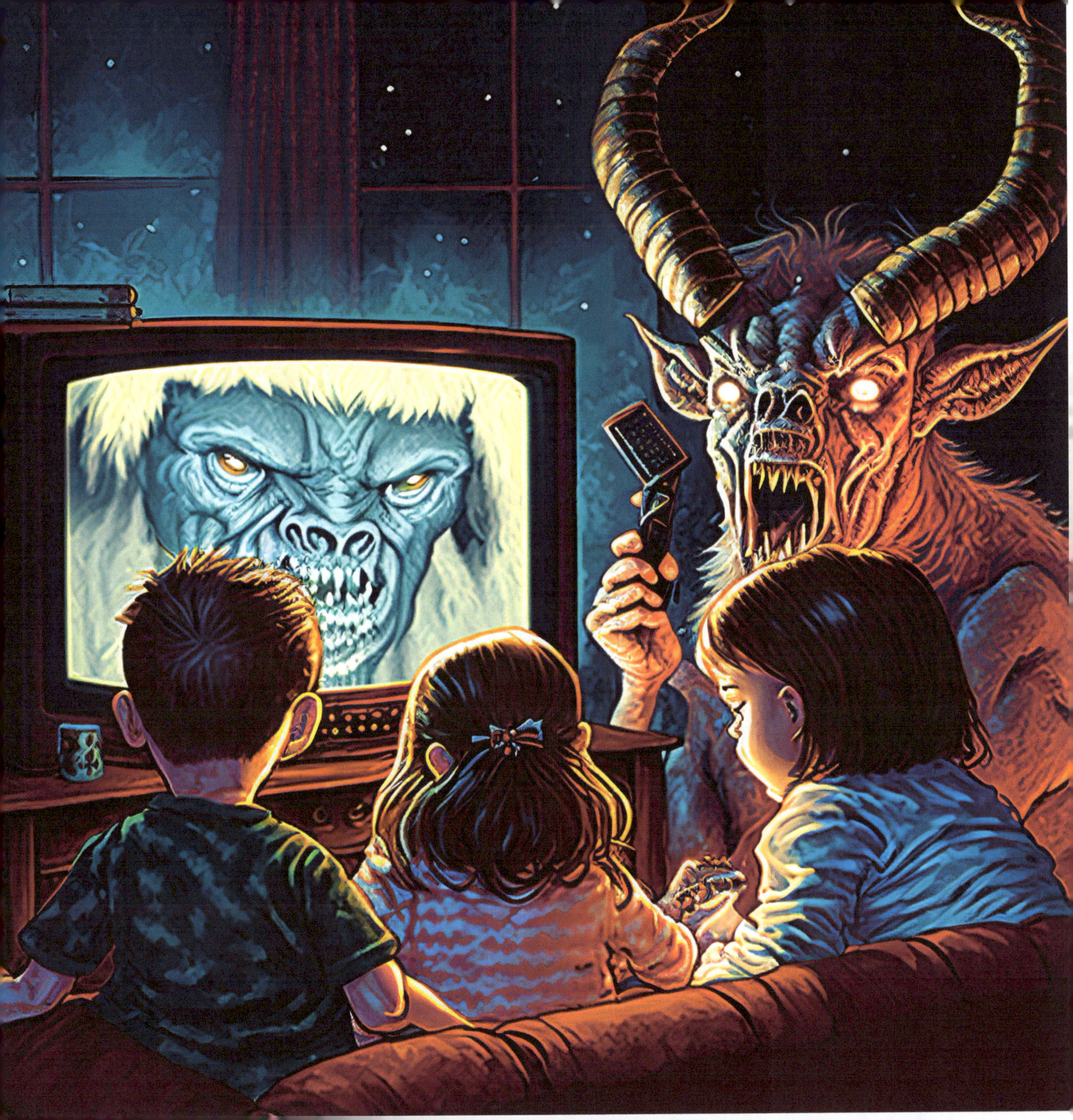

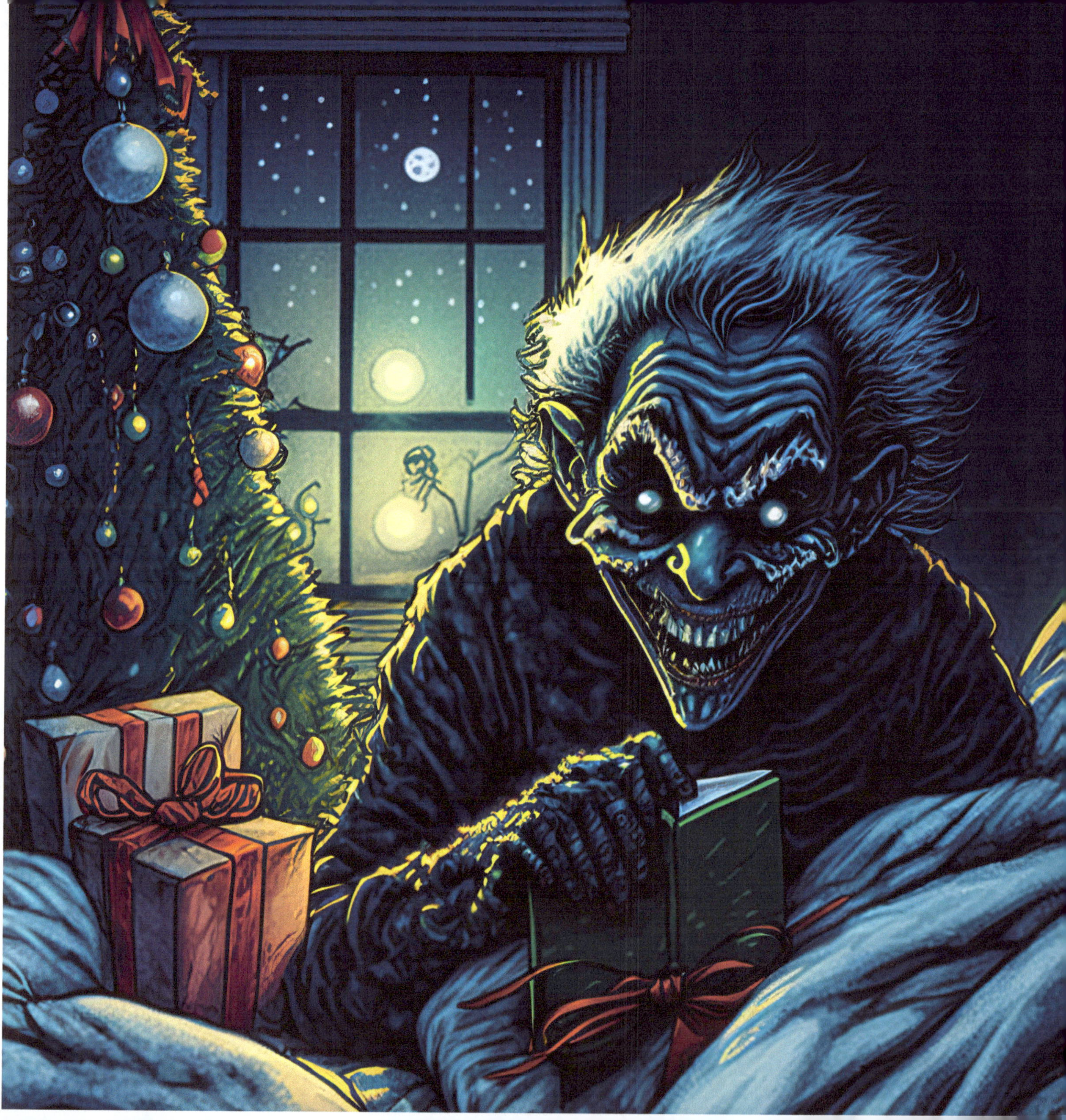

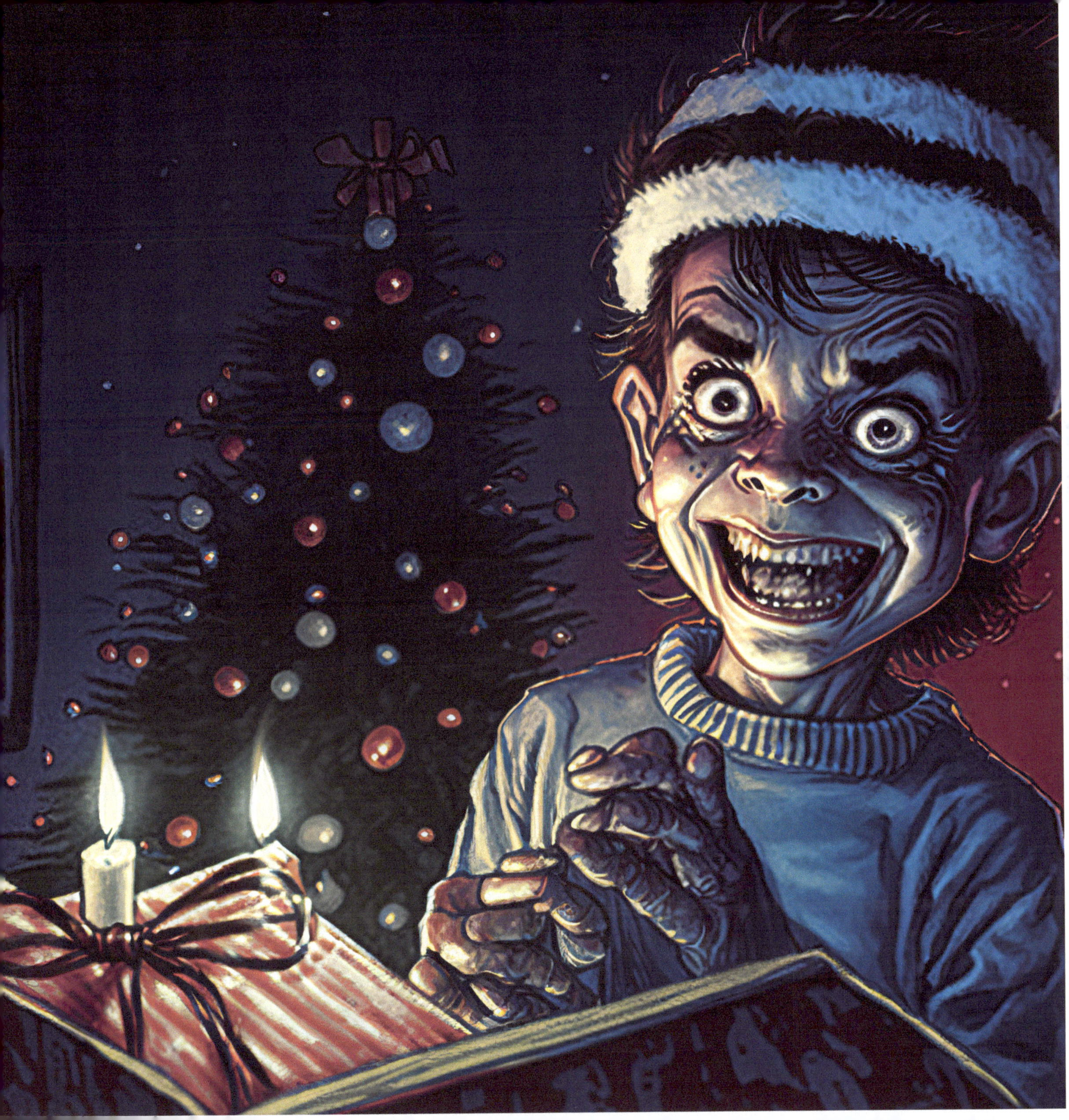

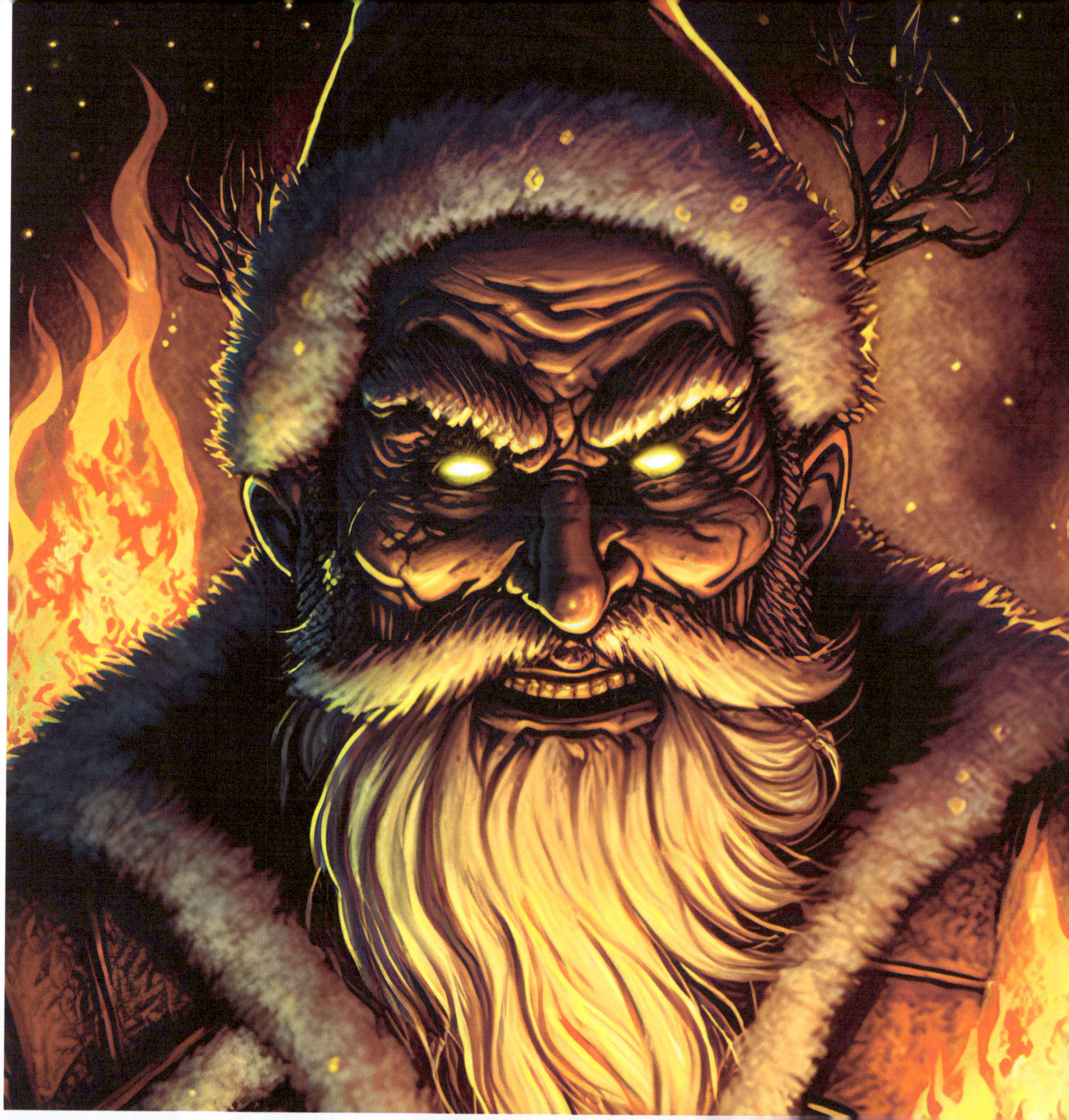

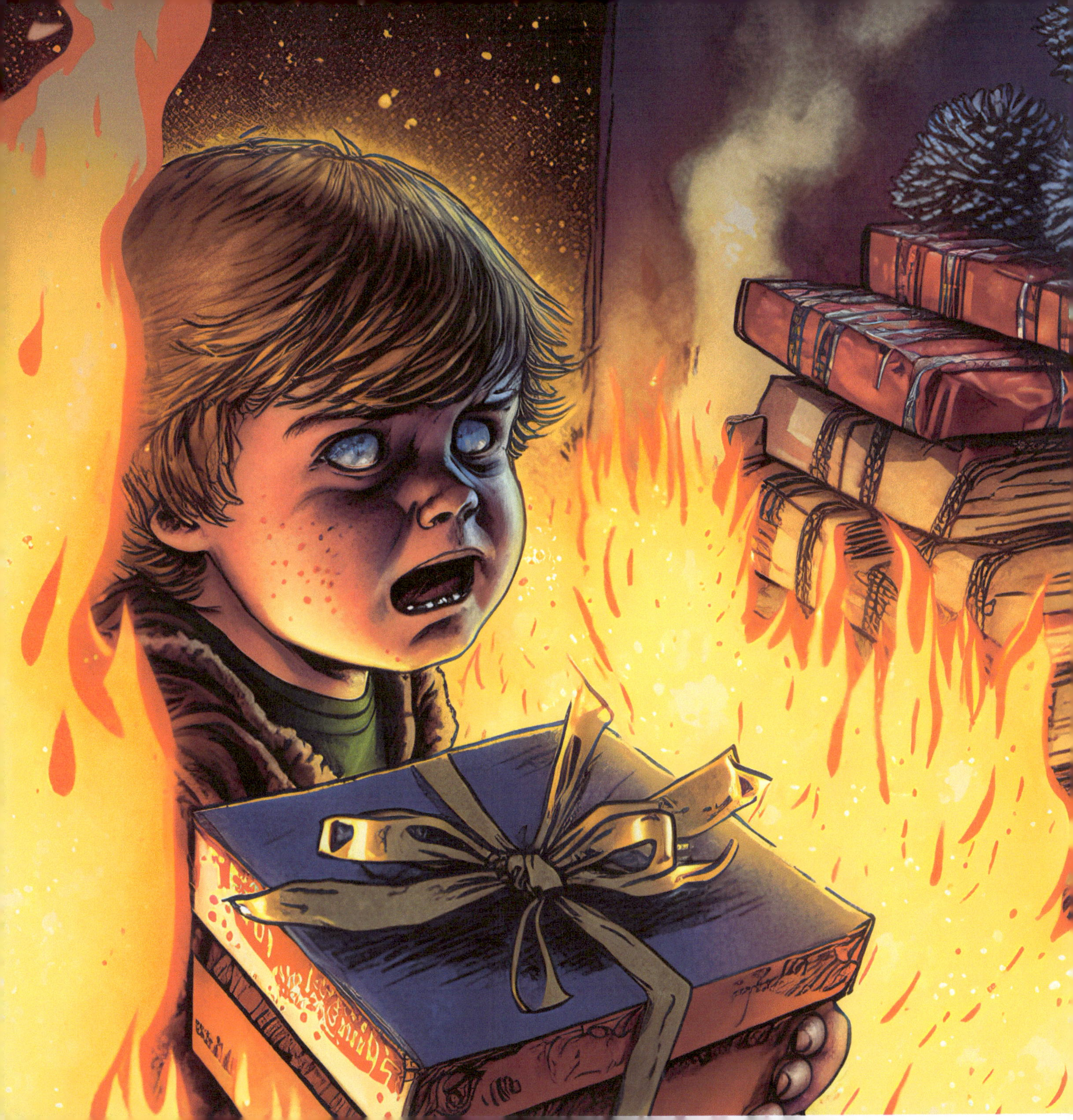

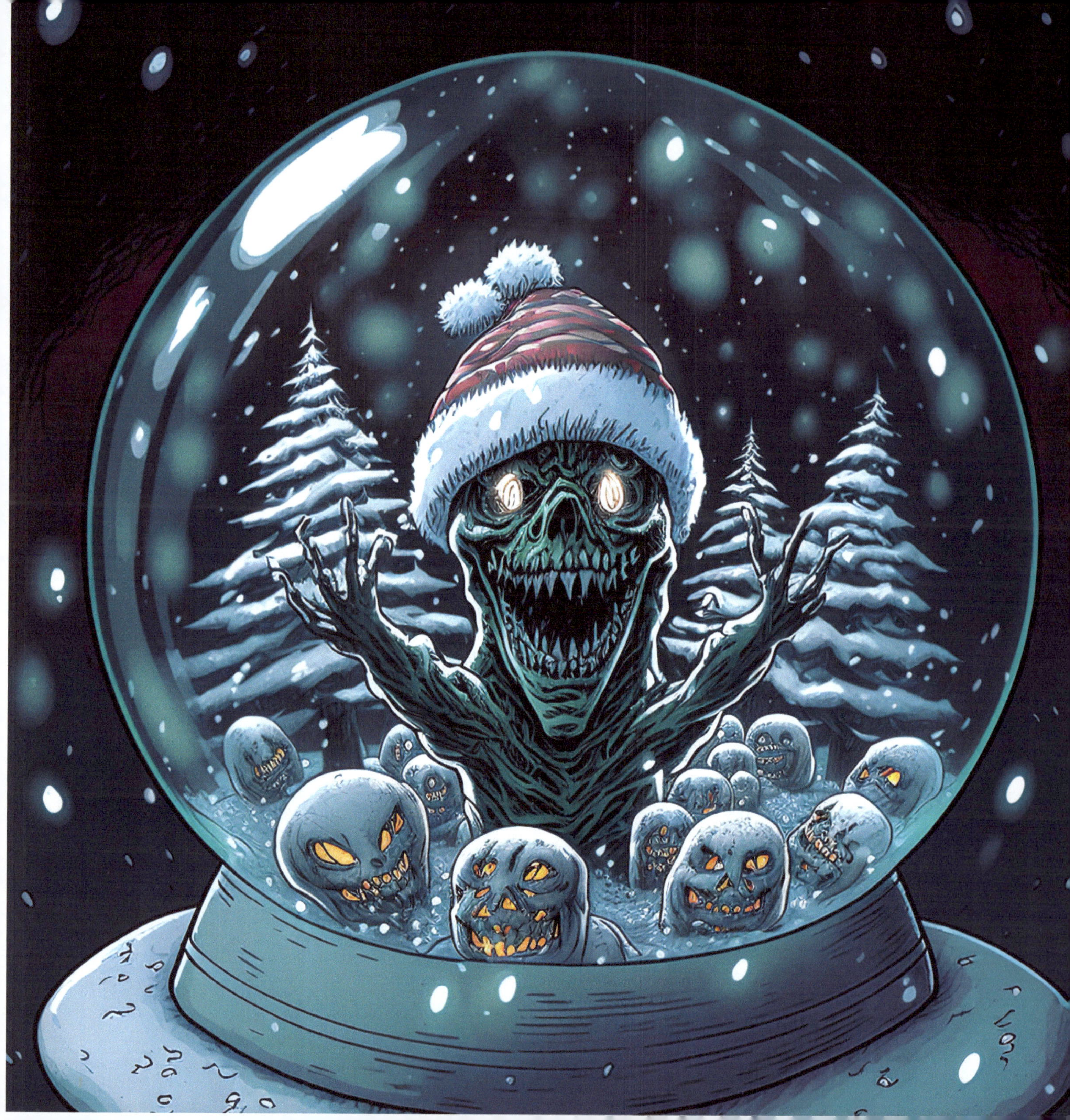

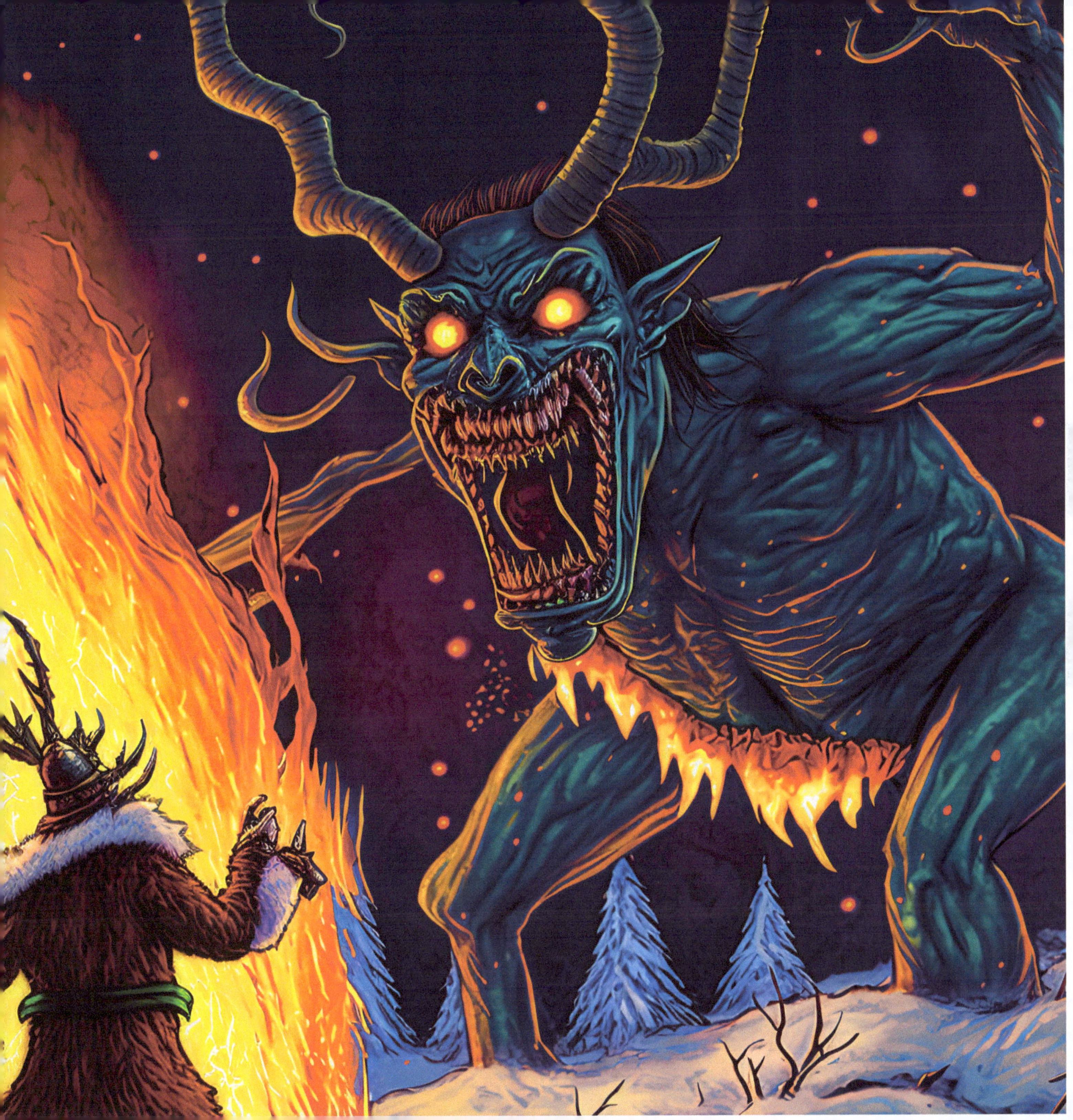

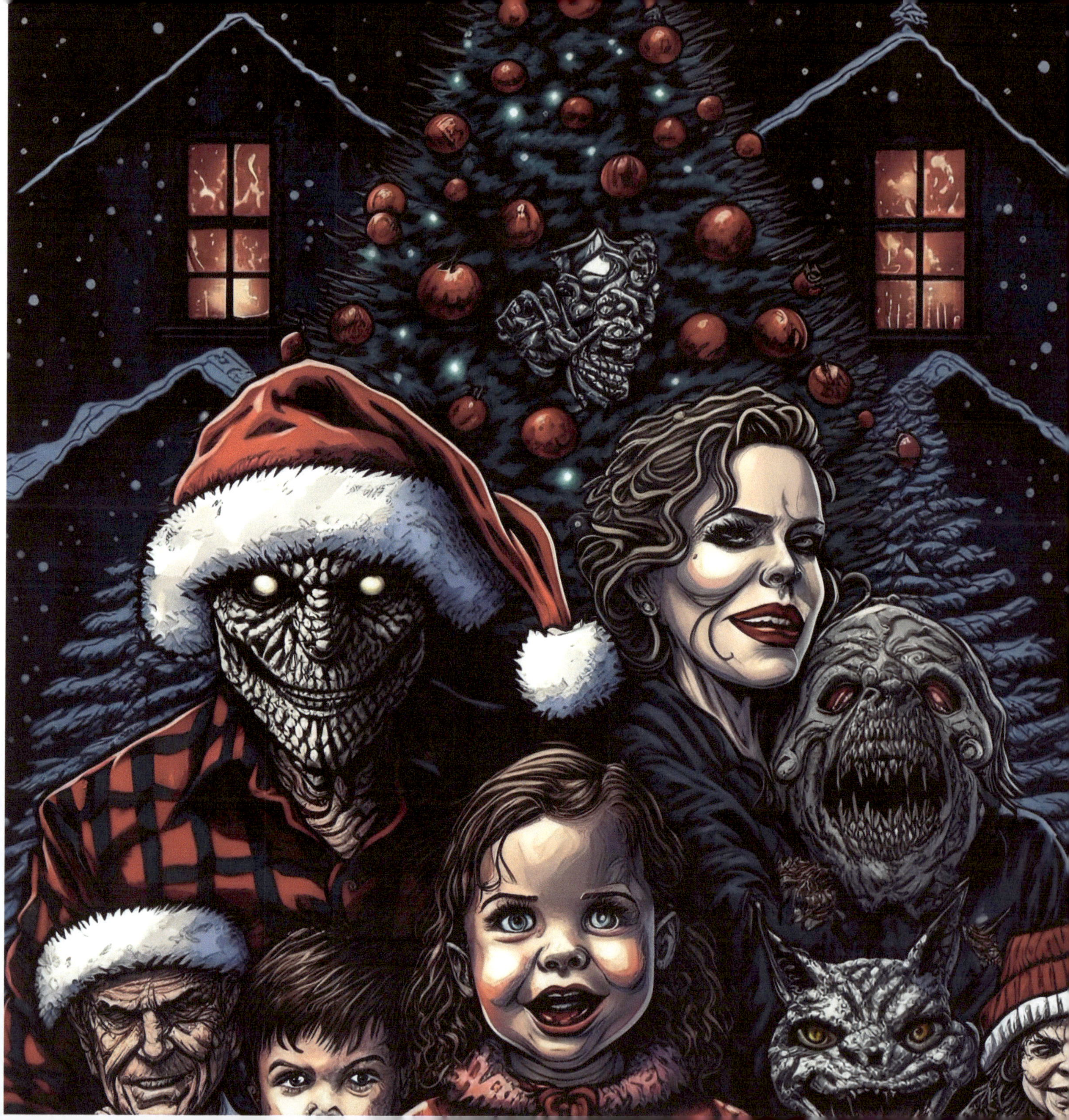

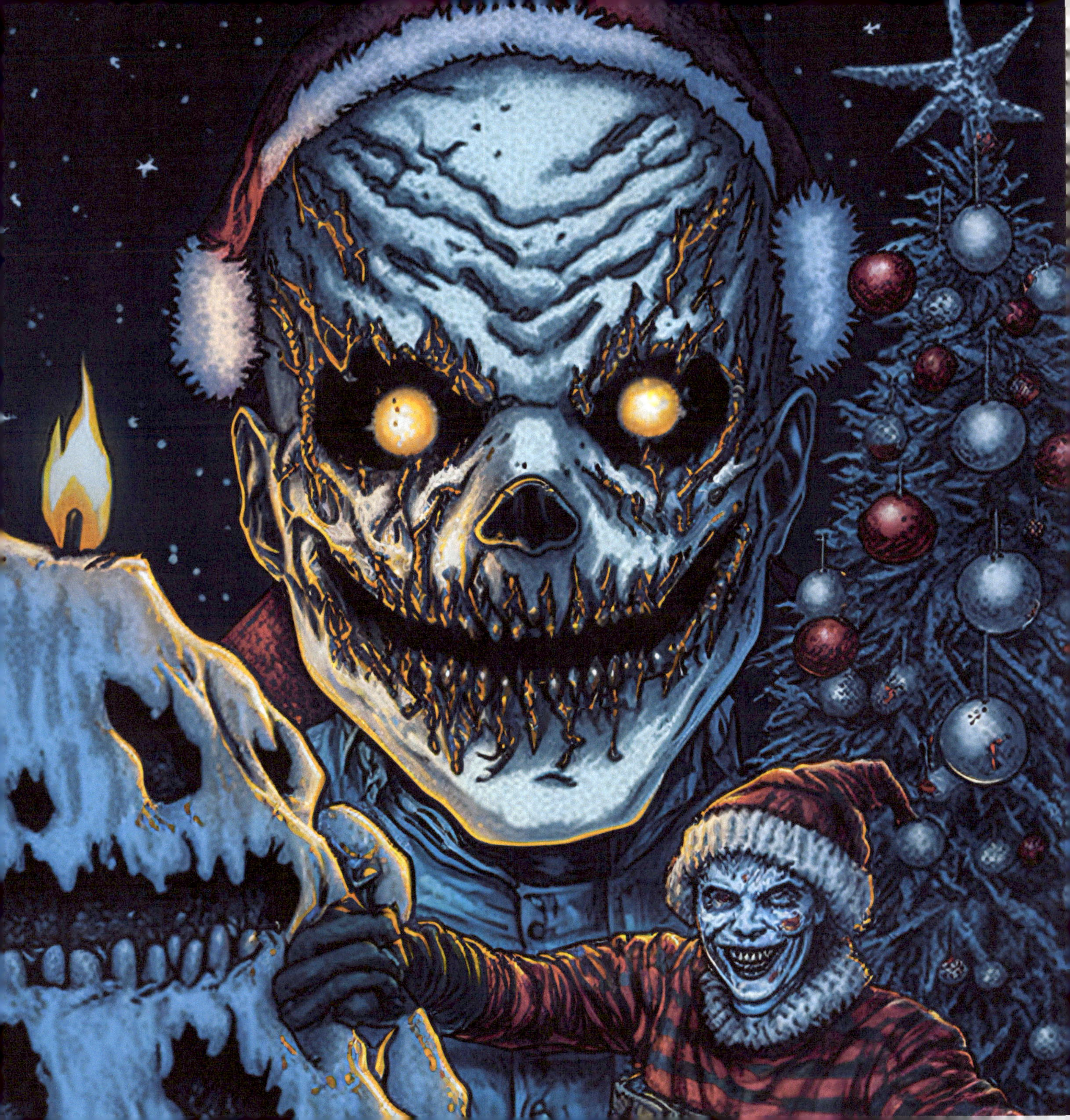

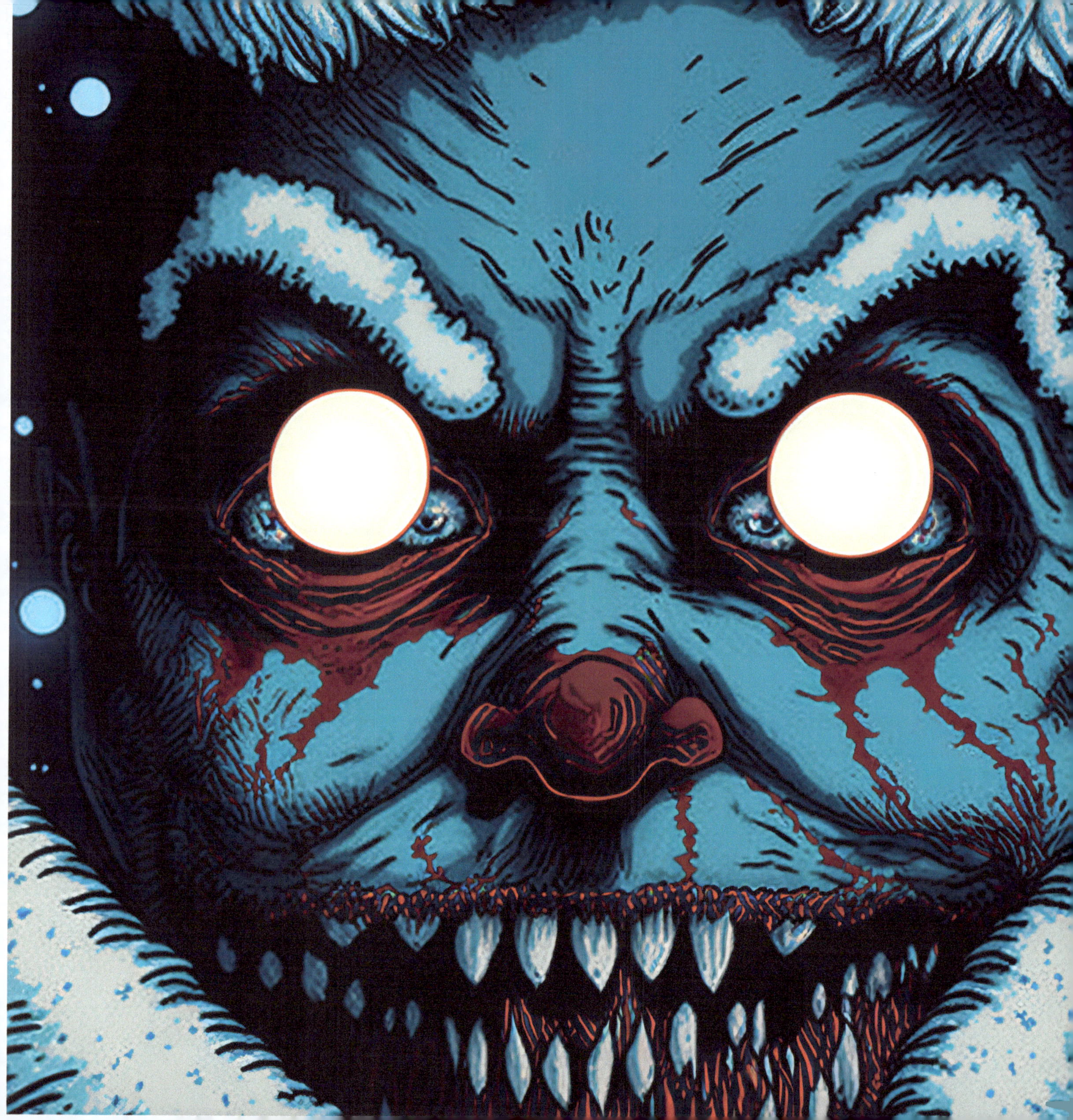

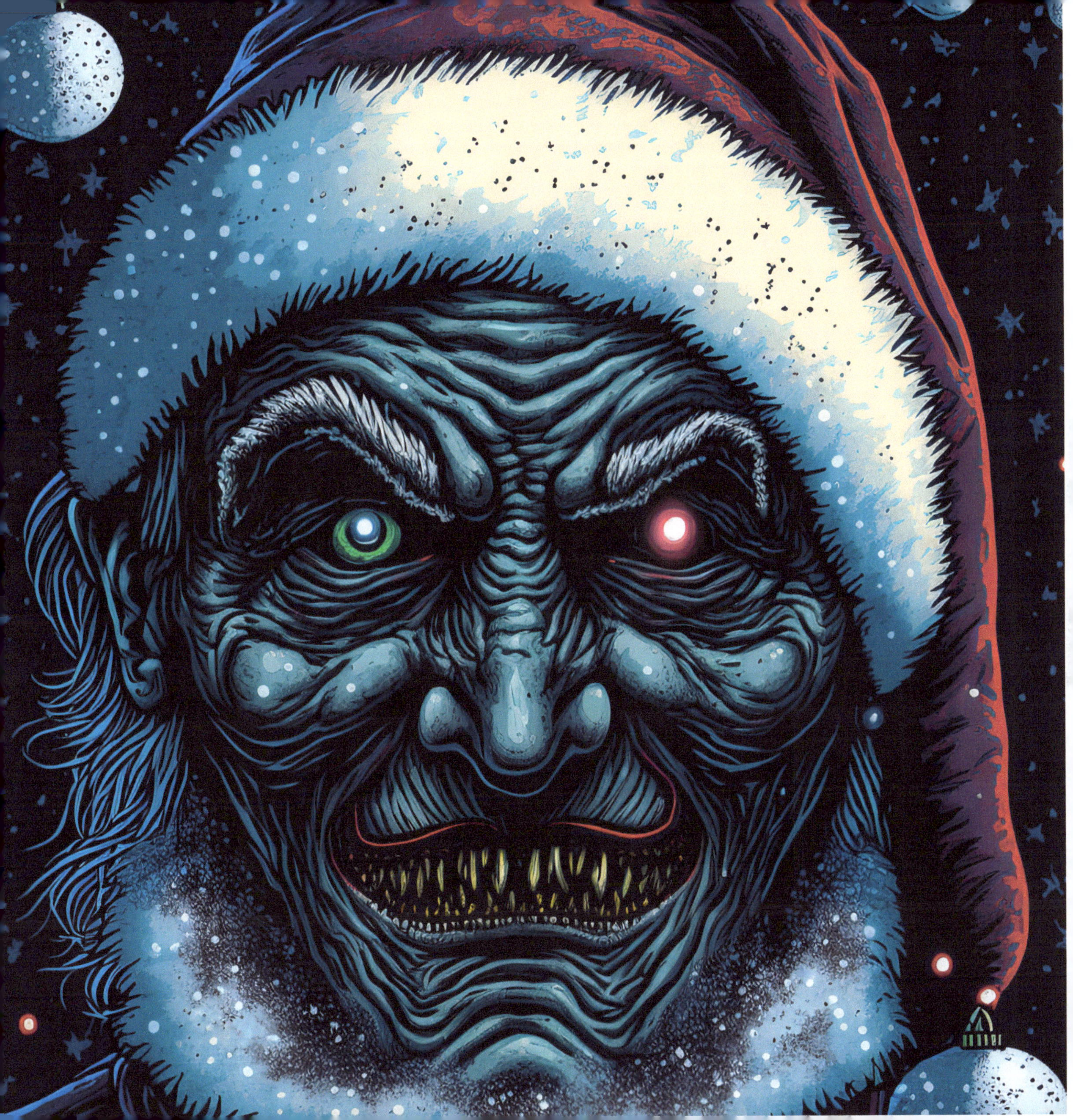

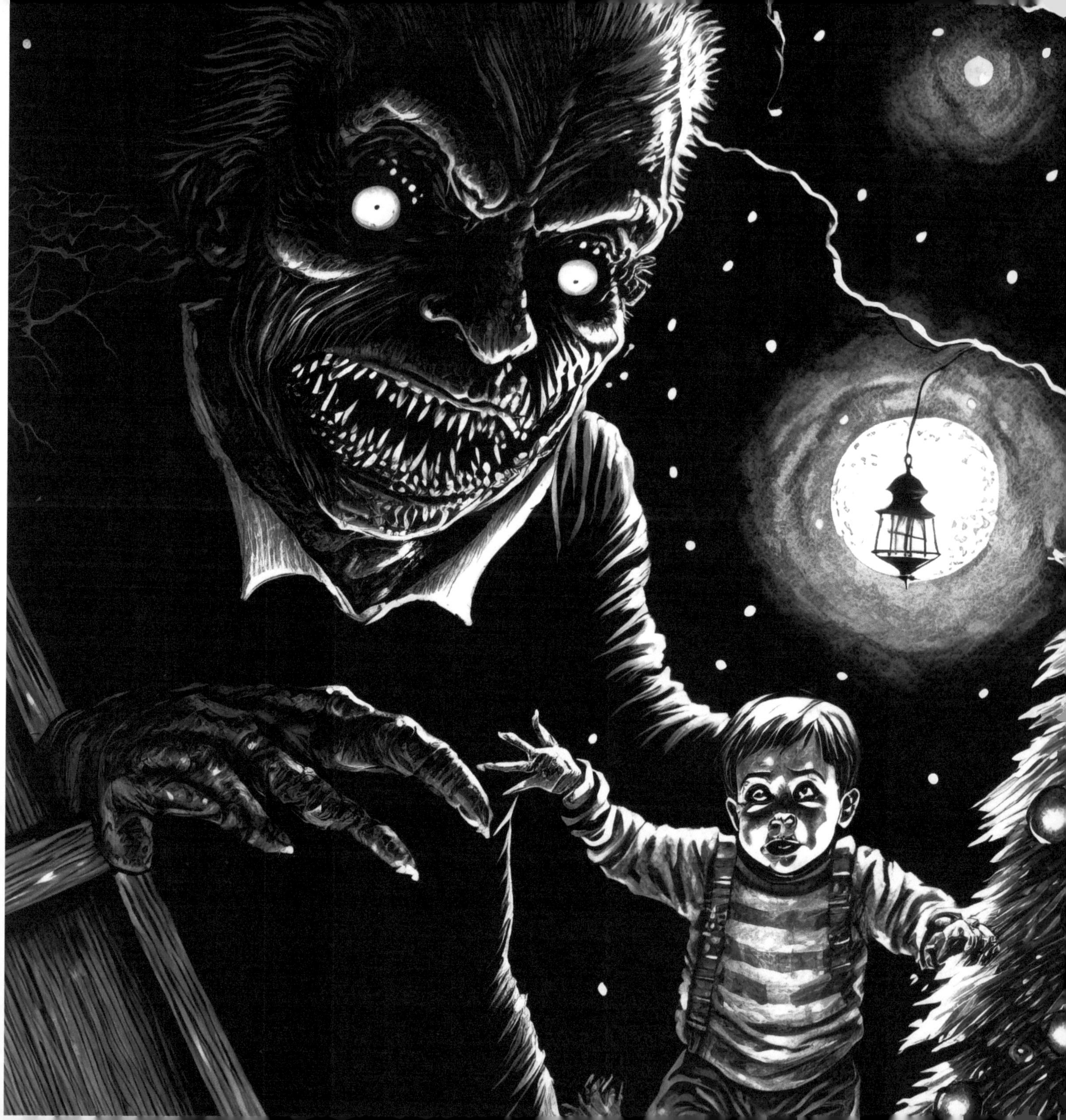

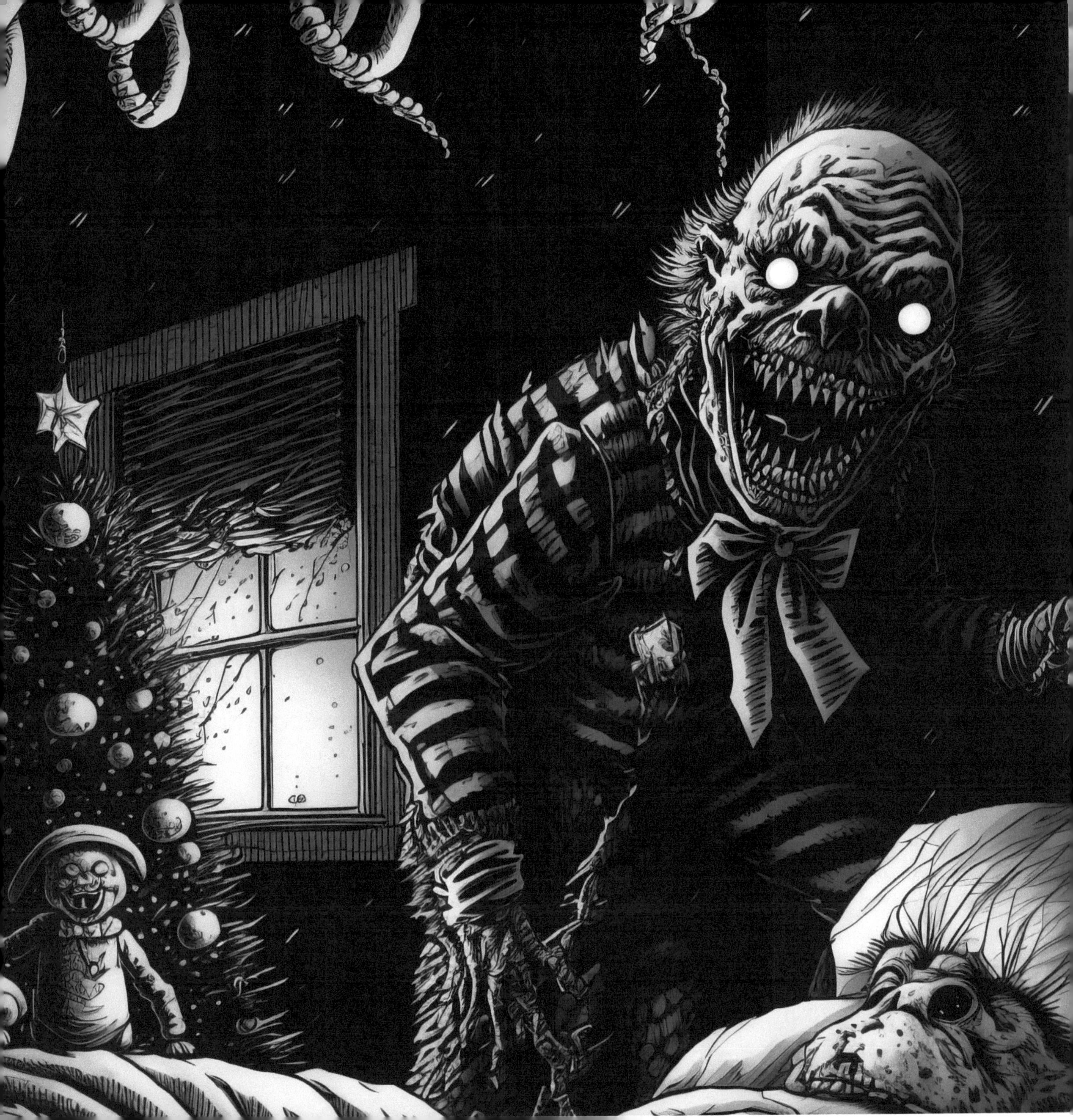

EPILOGUE

Every one of my projects always starts with the impulse
to create something I would want.
I've always loved Christmas and I've been a big horror fan since
I was a kid, so combining two things I love made sense.
And I can't draw, or at least not
at a level that I'd consider presentable,
but MidJourney allows me to create art that
I normally wouldn't be able to,
in exactly the style I loved growing up, when I collected horror comics.
And to me, this is the best use for new technology.
I hope you enjoyed looking at these creepy images
as much as I enjoyed creating them.

Merry Christmas,
DANIEL

www.ingramcontent.com/pod-product-compliance
Lightning Source LLC
Chambersburg PA
CBHW042050100726
47973CB00014B/205
9798218109202